TITANIC AFTERMATH

A Play in Three Acts
by
Michael Wehrli

Engelhardt Publishing
Portland, Oregon
www.titanicaftermath.com

BILLING AND CREDIT REQUIREMENTS

FOR PERFORMANCE RIGHTS

Please Contact:

Engelhardt Publishing

P.O. Box 820165

Portland, OR 97282

WEBSITE: www.titanicaftermath.com

E-MAIL: info@titanicaftermath.com

ABOUT THE AUTHOR

Michael Wehrli's other plays include *Found Lives* (based on the real life stories of Schizophrenia sufferers), *A Christmas Chaos, Dracula* and several scripts for youth audiences.

Titanic Aftermath was inspired by his lifelong fascination with the Titanic and all of its stories. He vividly remembers reading "A Night To Remember" by Walter Lord for the first time at the age of twelve. It left a deep impression and from then on he has continued to delve into the stories and history of the Titanic disaster.

PLAYWRIGHT'S NOTE

This play involves 21-25 actors playing over 110 roles. With the exception of the four primary characters virtually every line spoken by one of the survivor characters is based on a direct quote from that time period. It is suggested that this information be put into the show program, as it definitely enhances the theatre experience knowing that actual survivors spoke these very words. Furthermore, all the information and facts noted in the dialogue are factual, based on our current understandings. Note: all stage directions have been written in by the playwright.

It is also suggested that the following quote be put in the Show Program: *"There was peace, and the world had an even tenor to its way. True enough, from time to time there were events-catastrophes–like the Johnstown Flood, the San Francisco Earthquake–which stirred the sleeping world, but not enough to keep it from resuming its slumber. It seems to me that the disaster about to occur was the event, which not only made the world rub its eyes and awake, but woke it with a start, keeping it moving at a rapidly accelerating pace ever since, with less and less peace, satisfaction and happiness. . . To my mind the world of today awoke April 15, 1912."–Jack B. Thayer, Titanic First Class Passenger.*

ORIGINAL PRODUCTION

Dates:

March 31–April 16, 2000

Venue:

The Corner Theatre (DeSoto, Texas)

Company:

N. M. Productions Theatre Company

ORIGINAL CAST

PRINCIPALS

J. Bruce Ismay–Mark Hall

First Class–Pamela Stringer

Third Class–Irene Zuniga

Officer–Austin Von der Hoya

ENSEMBLE

Phillip Davis, Kelli Hagen, Jill Hall, Shane Hurst, Alex Klooster, Susan Klooster, Linda Kurosky, Dwight Murr, J.R. Peacock, Patrick Shackleford, Bobby Shue.

CREW

Director–Michael Wehrli

Stage Manager–Amy Pingel

Technical Director & Set Design–Damon Steele

Lighting Design–Kristina Denapolis

Costume Designer–Svea Hunt

Stage Crew & Dresser–Tara Adams

Box Office–Dolores Cole

Press Photography–Buddy Myers

WEBSITE–WWW.TITANICAFTERMATH.COM

CAST

PRINCIPALS

J. BRUCE ISMAY: Man. 74. Owner of the White Star Line at the time of the tragedy. Now near the end of his life and craving absolution.

FIRST CLASS *(Edith Evans.):* Woman. 30s. One of the only four first class women to not survive. Now a spirit who has come to hold Ismay accountable.

THIRD CLASS: Woman 20s. Another casualty of the tragedy who has sought out Ismay to take responsibility for his part of the disaster and the treatment of the third class passengers.

OFFICER: *(James P. Moody.):* Man. 20s. Also lost during the tragedy and wishes to have the truth exposed regarding the company's role in the disaster.

ENSEMBLE

Eight-Ten Women and Nine-Eleven Men playing 110 roles.

Details for suggested casting can be found at the end of the script.

THE SETTING

The mind and heart of J. Bruce Ismay. The stage should have a variety of levels with a few areas that are vaguely in the shape of a Lifeboat. One area should have a ramp at an extreme angle (or be able to shift to an angle). Fabric should be hanging at various angles all over the stage. The overall effect should be haunting and allow many entrance possibilities for the actors. Scrim may also be used for certain effects. Slides are used during the show to represent people who did not survive the disaster. Typically they are portrayed with voice over only. Slides can be projected on to the fabrics or scrim.

ACT ONE

AT RISE:

Intro MUSIC plays and leads into the below.

*(LIGHTS slowly come up to dimly reveal **ISMAY**, isolated in a pool of light. The **FIRST CLASS** Passenger, **THIRD CLASS** Passenger, and the **OFFICER** are also on the stage in the background, in darkness. **ISMAY** is old and somewhat frail. He sits, deep in troubling thought. After a pause, he slowly rises, clearly upset. He does his best to compose himself. As he tries, a SFX Soundscape begins: We hear the hum of an engine, people dining and happily talking. We then hear a clear voice—that of **ISMAY** himself saying "We will beat the Olympic and get in to New York on Tuesday." **ISMAY** winces. SFX continues during below.)*

ISMAY. *(Muttering to himself.)* My crowning achievement...

(SFX soundscape shifts into the sounds of the ship hitting the iceberg followed by sounds of people talking and running about in distress. ISMAY becomes agitated. We hear the voice of CAPTAIN SMITH saying "The ship is seriously damaged. It is going to founder . . . " SFX continue during below.)

ISMAY. *(Muttering to himself.)* No. It is not possible . . .

(SFX soundscape shifts again into the sounds of people panicking, horrible ship breaking noises. ISMAY becomes very agitated.)

ISMAY. There is nothing I could have done . . .

(SFX soundscape shifts again into the sounds of people flailing about in the water and yelling for help.)

ISMAY. It was suicide to go back . . .

(SFX soundscape shifts again into the sounds of a creaking lifeboat, lapping water, then silence.)

ISMAY. That horrid silence . . .

ALL ENSEMBLE. *(Including those off-stage. **ALL** heavily staggered and in a ghostly whisper.)* Ismay. . . .

*(**ISMAY** reacts as if hearing the voices in his head. **FIRST CLASS, THIRD CLASS** and **OFFICER** begin speaking while still in total darkness. **ISMAY** makes his way to Center Stage.)*

FIRST CLASS. It was a playground for the wealthy elite.

THIRD CLASS. It was a place where human beings were called "steerage".

OFFICER. It was the worst maritime disaster in history.

FIRST CLASS. It was a tribute to man's self-importance.

*(LIGHTS very dimly come up on the **FIRST CLASS, THIRD CLASS** and **OFFICER**. **ALL** are staring at **ISMAY** as they speak. **ISMAY** reacts to each person. The below dialogue begins to overlap.)*

ISMAY. It was an end to my dream.

THIRD CLASS. It was doom for the huddled masses.

OFFICER. 1503 people lost their lives.

THIRD CLASS. More First Class men were saved than Third Class children.

FIRST CLASS. Not enough lifeboats.

OFFICER. Six un-heeded ice warnings.

ISMAY. It was unavoidable.

FIRST CLASS. It was arrogance and greed.

THIRD CLASS. It was sanctioned discrimination.

OFFICER. It was a catastrophe waiting to happen.

ISMAY. *(Loud.)* It was the ruination of my life!

*(They **ALL** react and look at **ISMAY.**)*

FIRST CLASS. It was . . . The Titanic.

FIRST CLASS, THIRD CLASS, OFFICER. *(Heavily staggered.)* The Titanic.

ISMAY. Titanic. A word I've not spoken in 25 years.

*(**FIRST CLASS** approaches **ISMAY.**)*

FIRST CLASS. Perhaps it is time you heard it again.

*(**ISMAY** is slightly startled, and then addresses her.)*

ISMAY. I forbade the subject in my household.

FIRST CLASS. Seclusion does not absolution make.

ISMAY. Absolution . . . Peace–

*(He crosses away and is approached by **THIRD CLASS.**)*

THIRD CLASS. Cannot be achieved by denial.

ISMAY. I . . . have not the strength to come forward and clear the heretofore vilified name of James Bruce . . . Ismay.

ALL ENSEMBLE. *(Off-stage. Heavily staggered, whispering to each other as if in gossip and horror.)* Ismay! That's Ismay. Etc.

*(**ISMAY** reacts.)*

FIRST CLASS. The true father of this horrible disaster.

ISMAY. How dare you!

(ISMAY pulls away. LIGHTS come up on three different areas revealing three NEWSPAPER HAWKERS. ISMAY stops when he hears the first one.)

NEWSPAPER HAWKER 1. Bruce Ismay: the Benedict Arnold of the Sea!

NEWSPAPER HAWKER 2. How is it that Ismay, above all people, was in one of the life boats?!

(NEWSPAPER HAWKER 3 approaches ISMAY and shoves the newspaper in his face. ISMAY reads aloud.)

ISMAY. "Ismay, whose heart is atrophied by selfishness, is one of those human hogs whose animal desires swallow up all finer feelings."

NEWSPAPER HAWKER 3. *(Pointing to the newspaper.)* Reverend Baker P. Lee, LA Times.

(LIGHTS shift. NEWSPAPER HAWKERS exit.)

FIRST CLASS. My goodness. What a difficult time you must have had.

ISMAY. You can hardly imagine, madam. *(convincing himself.)* But the facts speak for themselves . . . Yes . . .

FIRST CLASS. Is that so?

(ISMAY pulls away. He is stopped by the OFFICER and THIRD CLASS.)

OFFICER. Which version of the "facts" are you referring to?

ISMAY. *(Flustered.)* The testimony. The accepted information–

THIRD CLASS. Is not the full truth! It does not reveal the full tragedy and upheaval caused by the disaster.

*(They direct **ISMAY'S** attention to **LUISE KINK, EDITH BROWN, & ANNE SOFIA TURJA** who are in three different pools of light and look directly at **ISMAY**.)*

L. KINK. It was so terrifying and traumatic that everything in my life up to April 14, 1912 was completely obliterated forever from my memory.

E. BROWN. Memories of that night have given me nightmares for most of my life; nightmares in which I awake with the screams of the dying ringing in my ears.

A. S. TURJA. On the morning of April 14th of any given year I remember what day it is with anguish and tears. No one can truly understand unless they had been there themselves.

*(**ALL** three exit looking at **ISMAY**. **FIRST CLASS** approaches **ISMAY**.)*

ISMAY. Many were traumatized by the event.

FIRST CLASS. Including yourself?

*(**ISMAY** turns away.)*

(Brief pause.)

OFFICER. Do you remember April 18th, 1912?

ISMAY. The day we pulled into the awaiting harbor in New York . . .

THIRD CLASS. Pier 52 was filled with nearly 30,000 people all wanting to see Carpathia's arrival.

OFFICER. The world was hungry for the full story of the Titanic.

FIRST CLASS. But you, of course, were hoping to avoid the milieu. Simply spirit yourself and the crew back to England, correct?

ISMAY. I . . . We all needed time to . . . collect ourselves.

FIRST CLASS. To get your stories straight, you mean.

ISMAY. I beg your–

OFFICER. Fortunately, there was a determined white-haired populist Republican from Michigan, who had made it his personal quest to find answers.

FIRST CLASS. The exuberant Senator William Alden Smith managed to quickly pass a resolution to authorize a panel to–

*(LIGHTS shift. **SENATOR SMITH** enters at a different part of the stage and starts addressing the Senate Hearings.)*

S. SMITH. To investigate the causes leading to the wreck of the White Star Liner Titanic, with its attendant loss of life so shocking to the civilized world.

(He pauses, looks at some papers.)

ISMAY. Such pomposity! Nobody on the panel, including Senator Smith, was a maritime expert!

FIRST CLASS. Ah, there was no escaping it, Mr. Ismay. There were many questions to be answered.

S. SMITH. The object of this committee in coming to New York coincident with the arrival of the Carpathia was prompted by the desire to avail ourselves of first-hand information from the active participants in this sad affair . . . .

(S. SMITH.'S voice now softens and continues **underscoring** *the other characters' dialogue. ISMAY– 1912 enters during the below and is sworn in.)*

S. SMITH. We went to the side of the Carpathia with purpose and pity, and saw the almost lifeless survivors in their garments of woe– joy and sorrow so intermingled that it was difficult to discern light from shadow, and the sad scene was only varied by the cry of reunited loved ones whose mutual grief was written in the language of creation. This committee's course is guided solely by one purpose–to obtain accurate information without delay and to secure a proper understanding of this disaster. Now, Mr. Ismay, will you kindly tell the committee the circumstances surrounding your voyage, and, as succinctly as possible, beginning with your going aboard the vessel at Liverpool, your place on the ship on the voyage, together with any circumstances you feel would be helpful to us in this inquiry?

OFFICER. Senator Smith's great gift for rhetoric never ceases to amaze me.

FIRST CLASS. Indeed. But it was his tenacity and thoroughness that ultimately proved invaluable.

ISMAY. I found the man an overzealous bore.

FIRST CLASS. Really? Because he had the audacity to question White Star Line's role in the tragedy?

ISMAY. I do not care for your tone, madam. I told them from the very beginning we had nothing to hide.

THIRD CLASS. Nothing to hide . . .

ISMAY. You can not imagine the tremen– dous anguish I was feeling. The pressure...

FIRST CLASS. I suppose being the first on the hot seat wasn't too comfortable. But, as President of the White Star Line–and the man responsible for the Titanic's existence–it was appropriate, don't you think?

ISMAY. Madam, I–

(ISMAY-1912 dialogue becomes prominent.)

ISMAY-1912. In the first place, I would like to express my sincere grief at this deplorable catastrophe. Therefore, so far as we are concerned, we welcome this investigation. We court the fullest inquiry. We have nothing to conceal; nothing to hide . . .

(ISMAY-1912 continues on softly underscoring the other dialogue.)

ISMAY-1912. I am hopeful that the committee may be able to suggest ways and means for the avoidance of similar accidents in the future, and anything that I personally or that the company with which I am connected can do to further that object will be gladly done.

FIRSTCLASS.
(Clapping.) Beautiful speech Mr. Ismay.

ISMAY. Ahem.

FIRST CLASS. By the way, didn't it strike you as ironic that the biggest inquiry of the "Gilded Age" began in the East Room of the Waldorf-Astoria hotel?

ISMAY. Peace, madam.

FIRST CLASS. And wasn't that crystal chandelier gorgeous?

(S.SMITH & ISMAY-1912 dialogue becomes prominent.)

S. SMITH. In what part of the ship were your quarters?

ISMAY-1912. My quarters were on B deck, just aft of the main companionway.–

(Again, S. SMITH and ISMAY-1912 continue on softly underscoring the other dialogue.)

S. SMITH.–Did you have some business in New York?

ISMAY-1912. I had no business to bring me to New York at all. I simply came in the natural course of events, as one is apt to, in the case of a new ship, to see how she works, and with the idea of seeing how we could improve on her for the next ship which we are building.

THIRD CLASS. Actually, the largest and most luxurious suite on the ship.

ISMAY. As the owner of the ship, it was my prerogative.

FIRST CLASS. Wasn't the White Star Line bought out by J. P. Morgan? An American?

ISMAY. Yes. An Ameri–can...

(S.SMITH & ISMAY-1912 dialogue becomes prominent.)

S. SMITH. Were there any other executive officers of the company aboard?

ISMAY-1912. None.–

(S. SMITH looks through his papers and consults with someone.)

THIRD CLASS. I hear your own wife and children did not come with you?

ISMAY. They decided to spend their time on a motor holiday through Wales.

FIRST CLASS. That must have been a source of pain for you.

ISMAY. Not at all. They had planned the trip for some time. She was most insistent.

FIRST CLASS. Ah, I see. Business before pleasure.

(S. SMITH approaches ISMAY-1912.)

S. SMITH. Mr. Ismay, please enlighten us as to the construction of the ship.

ISMAY-1912. The builders of the ship were Messrs. Harland & Wolff and they had carte blanche to put everything of the very best into that ship, and after spending all the money they can on her, they add on their commission to the gross cost of the ship, which we pay them.

S. SMITH. You were content that they should build that ship at whatever it cost to build it?

ISMAY-1912. Yes, sir. What we wanted was the very best ship they could possibly produce.

FIRST CLASS. Except where safety was concerned.

S. SMITH. In ordering that vessel were there any special instructions with reference to her safety?

ISMAY-1912. Yes! We were very anxious indeed to have a ship which would float with her two largest watertight compartments full of water. What we wanted to guard against was any steamer running into the ship and hitting her on a bulkhead. The Olympic and Titanic were so constructed that they would float with the two largest compartments full of water.

S. SMITH. Would you regard that as the most serious damage she was likely to encounter?

ISMAY-1912. Yes, sir.

(LIGHTS shift. **ENSEMBLE** *freezes.)*

FIRST CLASS. Come now, Mr. Ismay, you didn't believe that.

ISMAY. I did at the time.

FIRST CLASS. I think not. Companies like yours had slowly stripped away safety features during the prior forty years. Extreme safety simply wasn't very economical, was it?

(FIRST CLASS *gets blueprints and uses them during below.)*

ISMAY. As I previously stated, we spared no expense–

THIRD CLASS. For luxury and grandeur!

FIRST CLASS. But you can't have watertight decks with grand staircases. Doors in transverse bulkheads–where none should be–provides better service to your dining passengers. A double hull takes away precious room for more passengers and cargo space.

ISMAY. Those features were simply impractical.

FIRST CLASS. No sir, they simply got in the way of more profits. No horizontal bulkheads in the coal bunkers to prevent flooding; watertight bulkheads running only 10 feet above the water line– Do you want me to continue? All these safety features and more had been in use since 1858.

ISMAY. The competition at that time was fierce. We were under extreme pressure–

FIRST CLASS. So in other words, it was all a calculated risk, wasn't it?

ISMAY. Perhaps. No, I would not say that. There were the automatic watertight doors—

FIRST CLASS. Only 12, sir, at the very bottom of the ship. That left over 20 more that had to be closed manually. And on that night, some were sealed and some were not. You know as well as I, Mr. Ismay, Titanic's safety features, contrary to popular belief, were not "state-of-the art".

*(LIGHTS shift. **ENSEMBLE un-freezes**.)*

S. SMITH. Can you tell us anything about the inspection, and the certificate that was made and issued before sailing?

ISMAY-1912. The ship receives a Board of Trade passenger certificate; otherwise she would not be allowed to carry passengers.

*(LIGHTS shift. **ENSEMBLE freezes**.)*

FIRST CLASS. Ah yes, the glorious Board Of Trade . . .

THIRD CLASS. Run by rich businessmen for the benefit of rich business men.

ISMAY. Madam—

FIRST CLASS. Fortunately, their regulations never got in the way of profits—until a tragedy came along, of course...

ISMAY. They governed and regulated as was necessary. Their efforts benefited everyone who crossed the Atlantic.

FIRST CLASS. Really? They were thinking of the passengers?

ISMAY. Well, yes . . .

*(LIGHTS shift. **ENSEMBLE un-freezes**.)*

S. SMITH. Now, this Mr. Thomas Andrews was—

ISMAY-1912. *(Interrupting.)* Mr. Andrews was a designer and one of the directors of Harland & Wolff. He also superintended the building of the ships. He designed the Titanic.

S. SMITH. He did not survive?

ISMAY-1912. No sir, he did not.

S. SMITH. Do you have any idea, in his designs how it happened that the Titanic had but 20 lifeboats?

ISMAY-1912. None whatever. I imagine that he was simply fulfilling all the requirements of the Board of Trade.

*(LIGHTS shift. **ENSEMBLE freezes**.)*

FIRST CLASS. Your former managing director had a different point of view, didn't he?

ISMAY. You are referring to Alexander Carlisle, I presume?

FIRST CLASS. The very man.

ISMAY. Mr. Carlisle merely proposed new Welin davits for the Olympic and the Titanic, which we had put on.

FIRST CLASS. He also had a total of forty-eight lifeboats on his original plans.

ISMAY. I– I do not remember that.

FIRST CLASS. Convenient. Well, surely you remember Horatio Bottomley?

ISMAY. No.

FIRST CLASS. Oh, truly you must. Remember, his plea to the Board of Trade–to have White Star Line provide more life boats on the Olympic and Titanic? It was less than a year prior to the disaster.

ISMAY. Perhaps I did hear–

FIRST CLASS. No doubt. It must have frayed your nerves; what with the Olympic's maiden voyage pending.–

ISMAY. The White Star Line was in compliance with the existing laws–

FIRST CLASS. Bottomly pointed out the existing laws were antiquated and dealt with ships up to 10,000 tons, not 40,000 ton mammoths like yours. But it was all for naught, the Board of Trade managed to pigeonhole the resolution.

*(LIGHTS shift. **ENSEMBLE un-freezes**.)*

S. SMITH. Do you recall how many ships have been lost during your management?

ISMAY-1912. The only two that I remember are the Republic and the Naronic.

S. SMITH. Where was the Republic lost?

ISMAY-1912. An Italian steamer ran into her, I do not remember where; I think she was about 36 hours out of New York.

S. SMITH. Do you remember where the Naronic was lost?

ISMAY-1912. She was never heard of after leaving Liverpool.

S. SMITH. For what port was she destined?

ISMAY-1912. New York.

*(LIGHTS shift. **ENSEMBLE** freezes.)*

THIRD CLASS. It was rumored the Naronic struck ice.

ISMAY. What was that?

FIRST CLASS. Ice, Mr. Ismay. Tell me, isn't it true that speed, ice, and fog were the main perils to mariners at that time?

ISMAY. Yes, but that does not mean—

FIRST CLASS. And in the prior 50 years there had been twelve iceberg related disasters.

ISMAY. Madam—

FIRST CLASS. A majority of which occurred near the Titanic's grave.

ISMAY. Madam, there are risks in all modes of transportation.

FIRST CLASS. Ah . . .

*(LIGHTS shift. **ENSEMBLE** un-freezes.)*

S. SMITH. Did you have occasion to consult with the captain about the movement of the ship?

ISMAY-1912. Never.

S. SMITH. Did he consult you about it?

ISMAY-1912. Never.

S. SMITH. Did you have any conversation with the captain with reference to the speed of the ship?

ISMAY-1912. Never, sir.

S. SMITH. Did you, at any time, urge him to greater speed?

ISMAY-1912. No sir.

*(LIGHTS shift. **ENSEMBLE** freezes.)*

FIRST CLASS. Not entirely accurate, Mr. Ismay. Mrs. Elizabeth Lines heard differently.

*(LIGHTS isolate **ELIZABETH LINES** talking to someone in one pool of light. **ISMAY-1912** stands and moves to another pool of light.)*

E. LINES. I overheard Mr. Ismay and the Captain talking in the reception room on D-deck. As I listened, Mr. Ismay said:

*(SLIDE of **CAPTAIN SMITH** appears. **ISMAY-1912** turns towards the image.)*

ISMAY-1912. Well, we made a better run today than we did yesterday. We will make a better run tomorrow. Things are working smoothly.

E. LINES. He continued on in a rather dictatorial fashion, quite satisfied with the Titanic's performance, while Captain Smith only nodded. Finally, bringing his fist down on the arm of the settee.

ISMAY-1912. We will beat the Olympic and get in to New York on Tuesday!

*(LIGHTS shift. **LINES** exits.)*

ISMAY. I– I don't– I didn't think that information would have reflected well upon myself or the company.

FIRST CLASS. You are absolutely correct about that.

*(LIGHTS shift. **ISMAY-1912** sits. **ENSEMBLE** unfreezes.)*

S. SMITH. Was it supposed that you could reach New York at that time without putting the ship to its full running capacity?

ISMAY-1912. Oh, yes, sir. There was nothing to be gained by arriving at New York any earlier than that.

*(LIGHTS shift. **S. SMITH. & ISMAY-1912** continue on, pantomiming continued questioning.)*

FIRST CLASS. Well played, Bruce.

ISMAY. Enough, madam!

FIRST CLASS. I believe the Titanic was the fifteenth, wasn't it?

ISMAY. Fifteenth what?

FIRST CLASS. The fifteenth ship where 200 or more people died due to a ship—

ISMAY. I know what—

FIRST CLASS. Died due to a ship running at high speed through fog.

ISMAY. Fog is not an issue here, madam

FIRST CLASS. But speed is, Mr. Ismay.

(LIGHTS shift.)

S. SMITH. During the voyage, did you know, of your own knowledge, of your proximity to icebergs?

ISMAY-1912. No, sir; I did not. I know ice had been reported.

S. SMITH. Were you cognizant of your proximity to icebergs at all on Saturday?

ISMAY-1912. No sir.

S. SMITH. On Sunday?

ISMAY-1912. Sunday? No. I knew that we would be in the ice region that night sometime.

S. SMITH. Did you have any consultation with the captain or any other officers regarding the matter?

ISMAY-1912. Absolutely not. It was absolutely out of my province. I am not a navigator. I was simply a passenger on board the ship.

(LIGHTS shift. **ENSEMBLE freezes.***)*

FIRST CLASS. Ah-ah! When you were recalled several days later you had a different story to tell.

(LIGHTS shift. **ENSEMBLE un-freezes.***)*

S. SMITH. Mr. Ismay, I believe some passengers state that Captain Smith gave you a telegram reporting ice.

ISMAY-1912. Yes, sir, on Sunday afternoon, I think it was.

S. SMITH. What became of that telegram?

ISMAY-1912. I handed it back to Captain Smith, I should think about 7:10 on Sunday evening.

(SLIDE of **CAPTAIN SMITH.** *LIGHTS isolate* **ISMAY-1912** *who stands as does* **ISMAY.** *Both face the image of* **CAPTAIN SMITH.***)*

CAPTAIN SMITH. *(VOICE OVER.)* By the way, sir, have you got that telegram which I gave you this afternoon?

ISMAY-1912 and **ISMAY.** Yes.

CAPTAIN SMITH. *(VOICE OVER.)* I want it to put up in the officers' chart room.

(ISMAY-1912 sits. LIGHTS shift back to Hearing.)

ISMAY-1912. That is the only conversation I had with him in regard to the telegram. When he handed it to me, he made no remark at all.

*(LIGHTS shift. **S. SMITH.** & **ISMAY-1912** continue on, pantomiming continued questioning.)*

ISMAY. I would hardly call that "consulting" with him.

FIRST CLASS. Very well. Do your remember this interchange from your second round of testimony?

(LIGHTS shift back to Hearing.)

S. SMITH. Did you have any conversation with a passenger about slackening or increasing speed when you heard of the ice?

ISMAY-1912. No, sir; not that I have any recollection of. I presume you refer to what Mrs. Emily Ryerson said—

*(LIGHTS shift, isolating **ISMAY-1912** who rises. LIGHTS isolate **MRS. RYERSON** who faces **ISMAY-1912.**)*

MRS. RYERSON. Sunday afternoon Mr. Ismay, whom I know very slightly, passed me on the deck. He showed me, in his brusque manner, a Marconigram, saying—

*(**MRS. RYERSON** crosses to **ISMAY-1912.**)*

ISMAY-1912. We have just had news that we are in the iceberg area.

MRS. RYERSON. Of course, you will slow down.

ISMAY-1912. Oh, no, we will put on more boilers and get out of it.

*(LIGHTS shift back to Hearing. **MRS. RYERSON** exits. **ISMAY-1912** sits.)*

ISMAY-1912. Contrary to Mrs. Ryerson's story, and as I testified in New York, the day after we arrived, it was our intention, to run the ship for about four or six hours full speed to see what she could do, if the weather was satisfactory. That is all that occurred, sir.

*(LIGHTS shift. **ENSEMBLE freezes**.)*

ISMAY. My God.

FIRST CLASS. You were an excellent statesman for yourself and the company, Mr. Ismay. But let's go back to that first day of testimony; when the difficult questions began.

*(LIGHTS shift. **ENSEMBLE un-freezes**.)*

S. SMITH. What were the circumstances of your departure from the ship? I ask merely that–

ISMAY-1912. The boat was there. There was a certain number of men in the boat, and the officer called out asking if there were any more women, there was no response–no other passengers left on the deck. So, as the boat was in the act of being lowered away, I got into it.

S. SMITH. And you are sure there were no other persons around; no women, particularly?

ISMAY-1912. Absolutely none that I saw, sir.

S. SMITH. Who, if any one, told you to enter that lifeboat?

ISMAY-1912. No one, sir.

S. SMITH. Why did you enter it?

ISMAY-1912. Because there was room in the boat. She was being lowered away. I felt the ship was going down, and I got into the boat.

S. SMITH. Mr. Ismay, can you describe the manner in which she went down?

ISMAY-1912. I did not see her go down. I was sitting with my back to the ship. I was rowing all the time I was in the boat. We were pulling away.

S. SMITH. You were rowing?

ISMAY-1912. Yes; I did not wish to see her go down. I am glad I did not.

S. SMITH. When you last saw her, were there indications that she had broken in two?

ISMAY-1912. No, sir.

(LIGHTS shift. **ENSEMBLE** *freezes.)*

THIRD CLASS. Oh, but your precious ship did break in half, didn't it?

(LIGHTS isolate **MR. G. CROWE, MRS. WHITE, D. BUCKLEY** *and* **BULEY.***)*

MR. G. CROWE. The ship broke clean in two.

MRS. WHITE. In my opinion when it went down it was broken in two.

D. BUCKLEY. Yes, the ship broke in half. It made a terrible noise, like thunder.

E. BULEY. She snapped in two, and the bow part went down. We could see the afterpart afloat, and there was no forepart to it. We thought that maybe the afterpart would float altogether. But, she up righted herself for about five minutes, and then tipped over, went down headforemost and disappeared.

(LIGHTS shift. **MR. CROWE, MRS. WHITE, D. BUCKLEY** *and* **E. BULEY** *exit.)*

ISMAY. That could not be proven at the time.

THIRD CLASS. No it couldn't. But both Inquiries ignored the numerous accounts of the ship breaking in half and declared it had not–simply because you and the surviving officers said it hadn't.

FIRST CLASS. Fortunately for you, more than two miles of ocean covered many truths.

*(LIGHTS shift. **ENSEMBLE** un- freezes.)*

S. SMITH. I have a telegram here received by Mr. Philip A. Franklin vice president in the United States of the International Mercantile Marine Company, owners of the White Star Line. It is dated April 17, 1912 at 5:20 p.m., less than a day before you landed in New York. "Most desirable Titanic crew aboard Carpathia should be returned home earliest moment possible. Suggest you hold"–

*(**S. SMITH'S** voice trails off but continues to pantomime reading the letter aloud.)*

ISMAY. "–Suggest you hold Cedric, sailing her daylight Friday, unless you see any reason contrary. Propose returning in her myself. Please send outfit of clothes, including shoes, for me to Cedric. Have nothing of my own. Please reply. YAMSI."

S. SMITH.–"of my own. Please reply. YAMSI." Yamsi being your last name backwards.

ISMAY-1912. Yes sir.

S. SMITH. Judging from this and other messages, it was your intention to return the night you landed, if possible, to Liverpool?

ISMAY-1912. Yes, sir. At that time, you understand, I had not the slightest idea there was going to be any investigation of this sort.

FIRST CLASS. No doubt that was the furthest thing from your mind.

S. SMITH. When did you first learn of the investigation?

ISMAY-1912. Five minutes before I saw you, sir.

S. SMITH. Who informed you?

ISMAY-1912. Mr. Franklin. I think you came on board the ship with him, did you not, or about the same time?

S. SMITH. I followed very shortly.

(S. SMITH and ISMAY-1912 pantomime wrapping and exiting during the below. ENSEMBLE also slowly exits.)

FIRST CLASS. And soon after that, you were dismissed for the day.

ISMAY. Yes.

FIRST CLASS. That wasn't so hard, was it? Just a little whitewashing to help yourself and the company image.

ISMAY. You must understand the position I was in—

THIRD CLASS. "The position you were in"? Your "position" was hardly comparable to the agony wrought upon thousands of families.

ISMAY. I . . . I realize that.

THIRD CLASS. Do you?

(The sounds of mourning and weeping are heard Off-Stage. THIRD CLASS, OFFICER, & FIRST CLASS get close to ISMAY.)

THIRD CLASS. Did you hear the wails of mourning aboard the Carpathia?

FIRST CLASS. It began shortly after the survivors were on board.

OFFICER. And soon nature itself echoed the cries of the bereaved survivors.

*(LIGHTS Shift. SFX. Thunder & Rain. **KARL BEHR** comes rushing in. **ISMAY** and the others are watching, still dimly seen during the below testimonials.)*

K. BEHR. On our third night of the journey, it struck. I was asleep on a smoking-room table. I awoke suddenly to a loud crash and raced from the room; thinking the Carpathia, too, had hit an iceberg. To this day I feel a pull of terror during thunderstorms.

(Exits.)

THIRD CLASS. While you were hidden away in your private room, Mr. Ismay, there was an entire ship full of grieving, heart-sick women.

OFFICER. The few shattered men who survived were trying to keep a brave face.

FIRST CLASS. Everyone was at a breaking point.

*(LIGHTS isolate **EDWINA TROUT**.)*

E. TROUT. With the storm continuing, the thick fog, and the driving rain that kept everyone inside, it eventually became too much for me to bear and I simply went to pieces. It was months before I recovered.

(Exits.)

FIRST CLASS. Throughout the decks of the Carpathia were families searching to be reunited. In most cases, they met with despair and loss. Hundreds of women were forced to the realization that they were now widows.

*(LIGHTS isolate **CHARLOTTE COLLYER** She is writing a letter.)*

C. COLLYER. *(VOICE OVER.)* Dear Mother and all: My heart aches so I feel sometimes I shall go mad. I had not given up hope till today that he might be found, but I'm told all lifeboats are accounted for.

(Spoken.)

I wish I'd gone with him;

(VOICE OVER.)

If they had not wrenched Madge from me I would have stayed. But I know he would rather I lived for her little sake.

(Spoken.)

Oh Mother, I do not know what to do.

(VOICE OVER.)

Some have suggested staying in New York, others want me to go back to England but I can't.

(Spoken.)

I could never, at least not yet, go over the ground where my all is sleeping.

(VOICE OVER.)

Mother, I haven't a thing in the world that was his only his rings. Everything we had went down. God bless you dear Mother and help and comfort you in this awful sorrow.

(Spoken.)

Your loving child Charlotte.

*(LIGHTS dim. **C. COLLYER** exits. MUSIC bridge. LIGHTS shift.)*

THIRD CLASS. There was no escaping the sorrow.

FIRST CLASS. Unless you were J. Bruce Ismay.

ISMAY. An unfair assessment, madam. You have no idea what I went through. I was most distraught upon boarding the Carpathia.

FIRST CLASS. Do tell, Mr. Ismay.

ISMAY. Madam, I was not blind to the suffering!

(Composes himself and continues.)

When aboard, the ship's doctor urged me to come in from the cold and drink something warm, but all I desired was to be left alone. Somehow I found the strength to convince him to find a room where I could be quiet. He reluctantly agreed and took me to his own cabin.

THIRD CLASS. A cabin all to yourself!

FIRST CLASS. Where you stayed for the entire four days until you departed the ship in New York.

ISMAY. Yes. I never set foot outside the room. I never had anything of a solid nature, at all; I lived on soup. The fact is, I did not desire anything–other than solitude. But even that was denied me as the room was constantly being entered by people asking for the doctor.

FIRST CLASS. How tragic that you were the only male passenger to have a private room after the disaster.

ISMAY. You, Madam, are impertinent and rude.

FIRST CLASS. Perhaps so. But your safe haven did not keep you from the eyes of the world for long.

ISMAY. No, it did not.

FIRST CLASS. Actually, Mr. J. Bruce Ismay your seclusion may have seemed an arrogant use of privilege, but we know the real reason you desired to be alone, don't we?

ISMAY. What are you–

THIRD CLASS. It was to escape, wasn't it?

FIRST CLASS. A pitiful attempt to silence the dreadful sounds that haunt you to this day.

ISMAY. No–

OFFICER. When the Titanic foundered, over 1000 people were still on board.

THIRD CLASS. Most of those poor souls went with her. But hundreds more, were not so fortunate.

OFFICER. The water at that point was 28 degrees, and thanks to the well designed lifebelts, hundreds floated helplessly–

*(LIGHTS slowly shift. **ISMAY** pulls away, but everywhere he goes, he is confronted by an **ENSEMBLE** member–who enters right before his or her line. **ISMAY** grows increasingly more upset. Below dialogue should overlap slightly.)*

MRS. STEPHENSON. After she gave her final plunge the air filled with cries. We could hear their intense suffering from the icy water.

C.E.H. STENGEL. Then the cries began for help. There was an awful wail like. When I heard the cries I turned my back, I said, "I can not look any longer."

MAJOR PEUCHEN. Then the dreadful calls and cries: moaning and crying; frightful. At first it was horrible to listen to.

D. GIBSON. I will never forget the terrible cry that rang out from people who were thrown into the sea and others who were afraid for their loved ones.

EVA HART. The most dreadful sound of all is the sound of people drowning, the screams, absolutely ghastly. It was dreadful, dreadful.

MR. H. PITMAN. I heard the cries of distress, oh yes, crying, shouting, moaning from the water, after the ship disappeared.

MR. CLENCH. There were awful cries, and yelling and shouting.

ISMAY. No. No. No . . .

*(The **ENSEMBLE** slowly turns their backs as LIGHTS shift to extremely dim. **ISMAY** is isolated in a dim pool of light, alone. During **ISMAY'S** monologue, the **ENSEMBLE** keeps repeating the above lines–**MRS. STEPHENSON** through **MR. CLENCH**. They **ALL** say them at the same time, very quietly at first, underscoring **ISMAY'S** below monologue–creating an atmosphere of fear and foreboding. Slowly they start to build in volume.)*

ISMAY. The cacophony filled the night air with a power and depth that was overwhelming. Though my back was turned to the screaming masses, I could not escape the eyes of my boat mates–though few knew my identity. As it continued, the immense horror of the . . . accident washed over me. Accompanied by the unheeded pleas of the dying, my soul writhed–desperate for distance and seclusion. I thought: If only I can sequester myself away from these horrid staring eyes and the incessant doleful wails; perhaps then I can be counted among the "survivors."–

*(The **ENSEMBLE** are at their loudest point.)*

But sitting there, motionless, with the chilled air biting at my face and hands I felt as though I too was bobbing helplessly among the dying throng of people.

*(**ENSEMBLE** slowly fade out their voices.)*

As the dreadful wailing slowly subsided, I was struck by a macabre feeling of irony: my desire for aloneness versus the forced solitude of our situation. It is truly frightening to feel alone when you are surrounded by humanity. There was nowhere to go, there was nothing to do, but sit and wait.

(Silence. Pause.)

Eventually, we were both blessed and cursed when the silence began. The cold, dread quiet of . . . death. Not a word was uttered when the last of the pitiable cries ceased. It may have been hours or minutes, I cannot say. But truly that cloak of silence draped over my shoulders, and to this day I have been unable to shed its ponderous hold.

*(Pause. LIGHTS dim even more. MUSIC Bridge. **ENSEMBLE** exits. LIGHTS slowly shift. **FIRST CLASS, THIRD CLASS & OFFICER** cross to **ISMAY**.)*

FIRST CLASS. Quite a burden to carry for 25 years.

THIRD CLASS. Constantly replaying that night over and over again.

OFFICER. Forbidding your friends and family to ever speak about the Titanic.

FIRST CLASS. Living your life in relative seclusion, away from the high society you so desperately loved.

ISMAY. You cannot fathom the toll it took on my family.

FIRST CLASS. And yourself. Even your wife Florence said the disaster had "ruined your lives".

ISMAY. It did.

FIRST CLASS. Fortunately your forty million dollar net worth kept you comfortable.

THIRD CLASS. While most third class survivors lost everything they owned! They had to start their lives over in a strange country with nothing.

ISMAY. I did what I could to—

THIRD CLASS. You did what you could . . .

FIRST CLASS. I realize little of this was of concern to you in 1912. Especially with fine officers like Mr. Lightoller. He was invaluable in keeping the company, and you, free from blame.

(LIGHTOLLER and S. SMITH enter along with a few ENSEMBLE members. S.SMITH swears in LIGHTOLLER during below.)

OFFICER. Charles Herbert Lightoller, Titanic's second officer was a hero, Madam.

FIRST CLASS. No doubt about that. But at the Senate hearing?

OFFICER. He . . . He proved his unswerving devotion to White Star Line with his testimony.

FIRST CLASS. Yes indeed. A smart career move for a man expecting to command his own ship some day.

(LIGHTS shift. S. SMITH questioning LIGHTOLLER.)

S. SMITH. Were you present when the Titanic's trial runs were taken?

LIGHTOLLER. Yes sir.

S. SMITH. Please describe what they consisted of.

LIGHTOLLER. The trial trips consisted of turning circles and adjusting compasses. The weather conditions were fair and clear with a light breeze. The turning circles consisted of seeing in what space the ship will turn under certain helms with the engines at various speeds. She was put on a straight course for a certain distance under approximately a full head of steam. Then she came back again and was also reversed. The entire procedure took approximately six or seven hours.

(LIGHTS shift. **LIGHTOLLER & S. SMITH freeze.***)*

OFFICER. Only six or seven hours . . .

FIRST CLASS. Where most ships were tested for several days. In hindsight, that seems hopelessly inadequate, doesn't it?

ISMAY. We had a schedule to keep and clients clamoring to sail on the vessel.

FIRST CLASS. So why even bother with the perfunctory ship trials?

ISMAY. Without the trials the ship could not have received its certification by the Board of Trade to leave the port.

OFFICER. Evidently the certification was more important than fully testing the ship and its safety features.

FIRST CLASS. Thus, your company's last opportunity to avert disaster was lost to expediency.

ISMAY. Madam, I wouldn't–

FIRST CLASS. Oh, but you had customers waiting. So, you rounded up hundreds of unemployed men at Southampton to fill out the crew.–

ISMAY. You must—

FIRST CLASS.–Most of whom had never set foot on the ship before. Then a few days later, Titanic was on her way. Not the best way to ensure safety on a vessel, sir.

ISMAY. *(Pause.)* Perhaps not. Back then, the good of the company was foremost in my mind.

FIRST CLASS. And now?

ISMAY. Now? I would give anything to have that time to live over again.

FIRST CLASS. Good. But White Star's negligence was only part of the story, wasn't it?

*(**ISMAY** reacts. **FIRST CLASS** now turns to the **OFFICER**.)*

FIRST CLASS. There was also this hastily assembled crew, very few of whom sensed any danger after the collision.

*(LIGHTS shift to **W. H. TAYLOR, GEORGE MOORE, JOHN HARDY,** and **MR. JOSEPH BOXHALL** trading stories.)*

W. H. TAYLOR. A majority of the crew did not realize that she would sink. They were all skylarking and joking about it.

G. MOORE. I thought, myself, that there was nothing serious the matter.

J. HARDY. Everybody had full confidence that the ship would float.

MR. BOXHALL. I was quite undecided about whether the Titanic would go down.

*(LIGHTS shift back. **W. H. TAYLOR, G. MOORE, J. HARDY,** and **MR. BOXHALL** exit.)*

OFFICER. Captain Smith purposely limited the flow of information, so as not to cause a panic.

FIRST CLASS. Perhaps his only decisive action that night. Most people found him walking around in a daze.

OFFICER. Captain Smith and his ship had been given a death sentence. I say he performed courageously that night.

FIRST CLASS. Ah. But he certainly wasn't quick about it, was he? Waiting thirty five minutes before the first wireless distress call was sent.

OFFICER. It took a while to assess the damage.

FIRST CLASS. Then waiting another 30 minutes before officers asked Captain Smith to start sending up the rockets? Officers asked the captain if they could start loading the lifeboats, asked to lower them, and asked him to call the lifeboats back for more people.

THIRD CLASS. Which none of them did.

OFFICER. The Captain was keeping a cool exterior to calm the passengers and crew. Which was successful.

FIRST CLASS. Perhaps. But loading lifeboats to their capacity was not successful.

OFFICER. Most of the crew and officers were unfamiliar with the equipment.

FIRST CLASS. Ah . . .

*(LIGHTS shift back to **S. SMITH & LIGHTOLLER.**)*

S. SMITH. How did you reach a conclusion as to the number that should be permitted to go in?

LIGHTOLLER. My own judgment about the strength of the tackle.

S. SMITH. So, how many did you put in each boat?

LIGHTOLLER. In the first boat I put about 20 or 25. Twenty, sir.

S. SMITH. As a matter of fact it was not much more than half loaded, was it?

LIGHTOLLER. Floating capacity; no.

S. SMITH. How did it happen you did not put more people into that boat?

LIGHTOLLER. Because I did not consider it safe.

S. SMITH. In a great emergency like that, where there were limited facilities, could you not have afforded to try to put more people into that boat?

LIGHTOLLER. I did not know it was urgent then. I had no idea it was urgent.

S. SMITH. Supposing you had known it was urgent, what would you have done?

LIGHTOLLER. I would have taken more risks. I should not have considered it wise to put more in, but I might have taken risks.

*(LIGHTS shift, **LIGHTOLLER** & **S. SMITH** freeze.)*

OFFICER. All of us were left to our own wits as to the proper number. I thought 40 would be a safe load.

*(LIGHTS isolate **MR. LOWE** & **T. JONES** talking together.)*

T. JONES. According to what sort of falls there are. With good ropes you could take 50 or more.

MR. LOWE. It depends upon the caliber of the man lowering her and upon the gear also. One might say 25 or 30 while I might take a chance with 50.

(LIGHTS shift. **MR. LOWE & T. JONES** *exit.)*

FIRST CLASS. No one seemed to know that these lifeboats and davits were successfully tested in Belfast with the weight of 65 people.

OFFICER. None of us, including Captain Smith, were aware of that test. Harland & Wolff never told us they could be lowered fully loaded.

FIRST CLASS. The builders simply assumed they knew this as a "matter of general knowledge." Correct, Mr. Ismay?

ISMAY. At times, communication was somewhat lax.

FIRST CLASS. Yes, sir. And thanks to Captain Smith, the Titanic never held a boat drill. And most of the crew had never handled the davits.

OFFICER. That is unfortunately true.

FIRST CLASS. Of course none of that would have mattered had the Captain or officers been more cautious.

*(***OFFICER*** reacts. LIGHTS shift back to* ***LIGHTOLLER*** *&* ***S. SMITH.****)*

S. SMITH. The crew had taken several temperature readings from the sea that day and evening, correct?

LIGHTOLLER. Yes, sir.

S. SMITH. Showing the sea temperature had dropped to 31 degrees by 10:30pm that evening?

LIGHTOLLER. I believe that is correct sir.

FIRST CLASS. Always the careful answers.

S. SMITH. You knew you were in the vicinity of icebergs; did you not?

LIGHTOLLER. Water is absolutely no guide to icebergs, sir.

S. SMITH. I did not ask that. Did you know you were in the vicinity of icebergs?

LIGHTOLLER. No, sir.

(LIGHTS shift. **S. SMITH** *continues, pantomiming his questioning during the below.)*

FIRST CLASS. Oh really, Mr. Lightoller?

OFFICER. Remember, his primary focus was the protection of the company and fellow officers.

ISMAY. Yes.

(LIGHTS shift.)

S. SMITH. Did you know of the wireless message from the Amerika to the Titanic, warning you that you were in the vicinity of icebergs?

LIGHTOLLER. I cannot say that I saw that individual message.

S. SMITH. Did you hear of it?

LIGHTOLLER. I could not say, sir.

S. SMITH. Would you have heard of it?

LIGHTOLLER. Most probably, sir.

S. SMITH. But you received no communication of that kind?

LIGHTOLLER. I do not know whether I received the Amerika's; I knew that a communication had come from some ship.

S. SMITH. And it gave the latitude and the longitude of those icebergs?

LIGHTOLLER. No; no latitude.

S. SMITH. And that they were prevalent?

LIGHTOLLER. Speaking of the icebergs and naming their longitude.

S. SMITH. From whom did you get that information?

LIGHTOLLER. From the captain.

S. SMITH. That night?

LIGHTOLLER. Yes.

S. SMITH. Where were you then?

LIGHTOLLER. On the bridge.

S. SMITH. With the captain?

LIGHTOLLER. Yes.

S. SMITH. Did you slow up?

LIGHTOLLER. That I do not know, sir.

FIRST CLASS. Clearly you did not.

S. SMITH. You kept the ship on its course?

LIGHTOLLER. Yes, sir.

S. SMITH. And at about the same speed?

LIGHTOLLER. Yes, sir; as far as I know.

S. SMITH. How fast was the ship going at that time?

LIGHTOLLER. About 21 or 22 knots.

S. SMITH. Was that her maximum speed?

LIGHTOLLER. I do not know, sir. I could not say, sir.

FIRST CLASS. It was close to it.

S. SMITH. Do you know whether she went any faster than that at any time on the trip?

LIGHTOLLER. As far as we understood she would eventually go faster than that when the ship was tuned up.

S. SMITH. After you took the watch, Captain Lightoller—

LIGHTOLLER. I am not "captain."

S. SMITH. You have a certificate as captain, have you not?

LIGHTOLLER. Yes.

S. SMITH. Then you are entitled to the honor.

LIGHTOLLER. No; I do not claim the honor of the title "captain." I am plain "mister," as yet.

S. SMITH. Was the lookout increased that evening after you took the watch?

LIGHTOLLER. No, sir.

S. SMITH. Were you at all apprehensive about your proximity to these icebergs?

LIGHTOLLER. No, sir.

S. SMITH. And for that reason you did not think it necessary to increase the official lookout?

LIGHTOLLER. No, sir.

S. SMITH. What happened at the end of your watch?

LIGHTOLLER. When I ended the watch we roughly judged that we should be getting toward the vicinity of the ice, as reported by that Marconigram that I saw, somewhere about 11 o'clock.

S. SMITH. Did you talk with Mr. Murdoch about that phase of it when you left the watch?

LIGHTOLLER. No, sir.

S. SMITH. Did he ask you anything about it?

LIGHTOLLER. No, sir.

(S. SMITH looks at some papers.)

FIRST CLASS. His first major mistake.

OFFICER. Which he clarified at the British Inquiry.

*(LIGHTS shift isolating **LIGHTOLLER** at the British Inquiry. **LIGHTOLLER** stands. SLIDE of **LORD MERSEY. S. SMITH** exits.)*

LORD MERSEY. *(VOICE OVER.)* Was this an incorrect or incomplete statement?

LIGHTOLLER. Incomplete, I say, yes.

LORD MERSEY. *(VOICE OVER.)* And notwithstanding this evidence from the American Inquiry, you did tell Mr. Murdoch about the icebergs?

LIGHTOLLER. Undoubtedly, yes.

*(LIGHTS shift, spot on **LIGHTOLLER** becomes blue. **LIGHTOLLER** shifts his focus, puts on his hat. SLIDE of **MR. MURDOCH** appears.)*

LIGHTOLLER. We will be up around the ice somewhere about eleven o'clock, I suppose.

MR. MURDOCH. *(VOICE OVER.)* Thank you, Mr. Lightoller.

LIGHTOLLER. I've informed the crow's nest. The Captain wishes to be apprised if there is any doubt about the situation.

MR. MURDOCH. *(VOICE OVER.)* It shall be done. Carry on.

*(LIGHTS shift isolating **LIGHTOLLER** at the British Inquiry. SLIDE of **LORD MERSEY**. **LIGHTOLLER** shifts his focus, removes his hat.)*

LORD MERSEY. *(VOICE OVER.)* So then, the officer in charge, Mr. Murdoch, was fully advised by you that you were in proximity to these icebergs?

LIGHTOLLER. I would not call it proximity. But he was informed.

*(LIGHTS shift. **LIGHTOLLER** exits.)*

FIRST CLASS. It seems that the "proximity" of ice was well known.

OFFICER. It's true that a few officers and crew members knew we were to encounter ice at some time.

FIRST CLASS. A few?

*(LIGHTS isolate **MR. HERBERT PITMAN & FRED FLEET** sharing stories. **S. SMITH & MR. BOXHALL** enter on another part of the stage.)*

MR. H. PITMAN. We thought we might be in the vicinity of ice during Mr. Murdoch's watch.

F. FLEET. The men we relieved on lookout, told us to watch out for small ice, you know growlers and low-lying ice. Not as dangerous as icebergs.

*(LIGHTS shift to Hearing. **MR. H. PITMAN & F. FLEET** exit. **S. SMITH** is questioning **MR. BOXHALL**. **ISMAY, FIRST CLASS, OFFICER,** and **THIRD CLASS** observe and comment.)*

MR. BOXHALL. I did not realize the ship was so near the ice field.–

(MR. BOXHALL & S. SMITH continue pantomiming talking.)

FIRST CLASS. Not a wise answer from Fourth Officer Boxhall.

OFFICER. He . . . corrected his story later.

FIRST CLASS. Corrected?

MR. BOXHALL.–Of course I knew that we should be getting close up to those positions in the early hours of the middle watch but I did not think we should before midnight that night.

(S. SMITH dismisses MR. BOXHALL. Harold BRIDE enters. S. SMITH pantomimes swearing him in and then talking to him.)

OFFICER. Unfortunately the last fatal ice warning from the Mesaba, received at 9:30pm Sunday, never made it to the bridge.

FIRST CLASS. The very message that identified a huge rectangular ice field into which the Titanic was directly steaming.

H. BRIDE. Uh, Harold Bride, wireless operator. Mr. Phillips was working Cape Race and was inundated with passenger messages to send. I'm sure he meant to bring it to the bridge, but I suppose it got buried under his pile of work and never was brought up.

(S.SMITH dismisses H. BRIDE then looks at his notes as LIGHTOLLER enters and is sworn in. LIGHTS shift, S. SMITH & ENSEMBLE freeze.)

FIRST CLASS. If you had only studied the five prior ice warnings cumulatively it would have given a clear picture that we were heading straight into an immense ice field.

(SLIDE of Ice Chart.)

OFFICER. Now wait–

FIRST CLASS. See all those dots? They represent all the ice that was reported near the Titanic on April 14th. It's amazing we didn't come to disaster earlier.

OFFICER. Of course in hindsight–

THIRD CLASS. Why didn't Captain Smith pay more heed to these warnings?

OFFICER. Captain Smith . . . *(Collects himself.)* You must understand–to older sea Captains, like Smith, the wireless was just an interesting aside for wealthy passengers to send messages. Perhaps it could be helpful, but it would never replace his own experience.

FIRST CLASS. So it was complacency bordering on negligence.

OFFICER. *(Sighs.)* That is one way of looking at it.

(LIGHTS shift to Hearing.)

S. SMITH. Tell me, Capt–Mr. Lightoller, From six until ten o'clock was the Captain on the bridge at all?

LIGHTOLLER. Yes, sir.

S. SMITH. When did he arrive?

LIGHTOLLER. Five minutes to nine.

S. SMITH. What did you say to one another?

LIGHTOLLER. We spoke about the weather; calmness of the sea . . .

*(LIGHTS shift isolating **LIGHTOLLER** in a Blue Light. SLIDE of **CAPTAIN SMITH**. **LIGHTOLLER** stands and puts on his hat & faces the image. **S. SMITH** exits.)*

CAPTAIN SMITH. *(VOICE OVER.)* Quite cold, is it not?

LIGHTOLLER. Yes sir. Only one degree above freezing.

CAPTAIN SMITH. *(VOICE OVER.)* Not much wind, either.

LIGHTOLLER. No. A flat calm.

CAPTAIN SMITH. *(VOICE OVER.)* A flat calm . . . If the weather becomes the slightest bit hazy, we will have to slow down.

LIGHTOLLER. Yes sir. Pity there's no moon. Hopefully the breeze will kick up as we near the ice.

CAPTAIN SMITH. *(VOICE OVER.)* Hmm. Well, if in the slightest degree doubtful, let me know.

*(LIGHTS shift back. **LIGHTOLLER** and **ENSEMBLE** exit.)*

FIRST CLASS. So Captain Smith left the bridge to his officers knowing full well they may encounter ice.

OFFICER. Not an unheard of thing to do. He had an experienced crew—

FIRST CLASS. Most of whom had never worked together before. It was the Titanic's maiden voyage, and Captain Smith was very unfamiliar with handling a ship of that size.

OFFICER. He followed standard procedures—

FIRST CLASS. And by doing so doomed his ship! Captain Rostron of the Carpathia cared more for his vessel's safety. . .

*(LIGHTS isolate **CAPTAIN ROSTRON**.)*

CAPT. ROSTRON. Knowing that the Titanic had struck ice, of course I had to take extra care and every precaution. I doubled my lookouts, had an extra officer come to the bridge, and put an additional lookout in the eyes of the ship, that is right forward on deck. We exerted extra vigilance and every possible care was taken. We were all on the qui vive. *(French-"kee veev", means "on the alert, watchful".)*

(LIGHTS shift back.)

OFFICER. The Carpathia was coming to save the Titanic. Under those circumstances—

FIRST CLASS. He took extra precautions, didn't he? Even Stanley Lord, the much condemned Captain of the Californian, took prudent measures. And this was before he heard of the Titanic's catastrophe.

*(LIGHTS isolate **CAPTAIN LORD**.)*

CAPT. LORD. As soon as it became dark, we doubled the lookout, put a man on the forecastle head, and I stayed on the bridge myself with an officer. We were just taking the extra precautions. I remained on the bridge until half past 10. Eventually I decided to stop altogether.

(LIGHTS shift back.)

FIRST CLASS. Yet another Captain taking extra precautions.

OFFICER. Yes, he undoubtedly did.

FIRST CLASS. Want another example? Captain Moore of the Mount Temple, which also made its way to the Titanic. . .

*(LIGHTS isolate **CAPTAIN G. MOORE**.)*

CAPT. G. MOORE. In my book, under normal conditions, the usual thing on approaching ice, at night, is to stop and wait until daylight. I think it was very unwise for Captain Smith to have continued his speed when warned of ice ahead.

(LIGHTS shift back.)

OFFICER. All right . . . I'll grant you that if Captain Smith had taken extra care that dreadful night, the accident may have been avoided.

FIRST CLASS. Would have been avoided.

(Pause.)

OFFICER. Yes. Would.

*(**ISMAY** reacts.)*

THIRD CLASS. But that didn't keep Lightoller from continuing the "whitewashing" of responsibility, did it?

OFFICER. No . . . Especially at the British Inquiry.

FIRST CLASS. Thomas Scanlan, God love him, was determined to get the truth–

OFFICER. Of course. Scanlan represented the National Sailor's & Firemen's Union.

FIRST CLASS. A fact quite dismaying to Lord Mersey who was running that "show trial".

*(LIGHTS shift to the British Inquiry. **THOMAS SCANLAN, LIGHTOLLER** and **ENSEMBLE** are there.)*

T. SCANLAN. Would it not have been desirable to station more look-out men on the bows or the stem-head?

LIGHTOLLER. Anything which would be conducive to avoiding danger.

T. SCANLAN. Would that be conducive to avoiding danger?

LIGHTOLLER. It might be.

T. SCANLAN. I am speaking to you as a man of great practical experience.

LIGHTOLLER. I could not exactly say whether look-outs in the stem head would help. We do not place very much reliance on them; we hope they will keep a very good look-out, but you have not the same control over them as you have the regular look-out men in the crow's nest. They have nothing to sacrifice in the way of a good room, which the look-out men receive for their service.

(LIGHTS shift back. ***LIGHTOLLER & T. SCANLAN*** *continue pantomiming talking.)*

FIRST CLASS. Despite Mr. Scanlan's efforts, it is abundantly clear the entire British Inquiry did not care to discover the entire truth. No! They simply wanted to sanitize it.

ISMAY. It was a very unpleasant experience. I spent many hours on the stand myself.

FIRST CLASS. But you and your company were exonerated, weren't you?

OFFICER. Of course they were! The British Board of Trade was the very government ministry responsible for the outdated maritime safety laws. And they were conducting the Inquiry!

FIRST CLASS. So once again, the vested interest of those who had the most to lose were running the show. But Scanlan didn't make it easy for Lightoller.

(LIGHTS shift to the British Inquiry.)

T. SCANLAN. You were asked by my Lord this forenoon how an unfortunate accident like this could have been prevented in what you describe as abnormal circumstances?

LIGHTOLLER. Yes.

T. SCANLAN. Is it not quite clear that the most obvious way to avoid it is by slackening speed?

LIGHTOLLER. Not necessarily the most obvious.

T. SCANLAN. Well, is it one way?

LIGHTOLLER. It is one way. Naturally, if you stop the ship you will not collide with anything.

T. SCANLAN. Am I to understand, even with the knowledge you have had coming through this 'Titanic' disaster, at the present moment, if you were placed in the same circumstances, you would still bang on at 21 ½ knots an hour?

LIGHTOLLER. I do not say I should bang on at all; I do not approve of the term banging on.–

T. SCANLAN. *(Overlapping.)* –I mean drive ahead?–

LIGHTOLLER. *(Overlapping.)* –That looks like carelessness you know; it looks as if we would recklessly bang on and slap her into it regardless of anything. Undoubtedly we should not do that.

T. SCANLAN. What I want to suggest to you is that it was utter recklessness, in view of the conditions which you have described as abnormal, and in view of the knowledge you had from various sources that ice was in your immediate vicinity, to proceed at 21 ½ knots?

LIGHTOLLER. Then all I can say is that recklessness applies to practically every commander in every ship crossing the Atlantic Ocean.

T. SCANLAN. I am not disputing that with you, but can you describe it yourself as other than reckless? Is it careful navigation in your view?

LIGHTOLLER. It is ordinary navigation, which embodies careful navigation.

T. SCANLAN. What I want to suggest is that the conditions having been so dangerous, those in charge of the vessel were negligent in proceeding at that rate of speed?

LIGHTOLLER. No.

(LIGHTS shift. **LIGHTOLLER** *is dismissed by* **T. SCANLAN**. *Both exit.)*

ISMAY. What choice did he have?

OFFICER. In his mind, none. Apart from protecting himself, he knew the Board of Trade had no interest in seeing the White Star Line or its officers found negligent.

FIRST CLASS. Thus opening the door to millions of dollars in law suits, which would tie up the courts for years, and possibly break the White Star Line. Wouldn't that have been a pity!

ISMAY. Yes madam, it would. What you fail to realize is that economics played into every decision before, during and after the disaster.

FIRST CLASS. Ah, a glimmer of truth at last.

ISMAY. The economic reality, madam, is that high-prestige clients expect immense luxury and reliable travel times. Therefore we, as dutiful businessmen give them what they desire.

FIRST CLASS. That is not what is being disputed!

ISMAY. I understand that. In regards to the accident and its preventability, I . . . I do agree that more precautions could have been taken.

FIRST CLASS. Yes, they should have.

ISMAY. However–

FIRST CLASS. There is no–

ISMAY. Let me finish, Madam. We did take into account innumerable factors when designing the ship: safety, weather conditions, wireless communication, and so on. At the time, we were convinced the risks were infinitesimally small. Obviously in hindsight, we were terribly wrong.

FIRST CLASS. Isn't that always the case in disasters of this magnitude? It's only after the fact that human life is the top priority.

(ISMAY reacts. Pause.)

OFFICER. Officer Lightoller revealed his true feelings many years after the Inquiries.

*(LIGHTS isolate **OLDER LIGHTOLLER** talking to an **ENSEMBLE** member as an Interviewer.)*

OLDER LIGHTOLLER. In Washington it was of little consequence, but in London it was very necessary to keep one's hands on the whitewash brush. A washing of dirty linen would help no one, though in all conscience it was a difficult task. When one had known, full well, and for many years, the ever-present possibility of just such a disaster. They chose me as their whipping boy and nearly pulled my hide off completely, each one seemed to want his bit. But I think in the end the Board of Trade and the White Star Line won.

(LIGHTS shift back.)

FIRST CLASS. And following in the company's footsteps, Captain Smith maintained speed and—

OFFICER. The Captain did the best he could with the expectations and regulations at hand.

FIRST CLASS. But he did nothing above and beyond that! On a moonless night with a calm sea and several ice warnings, he did not slow down, did not post extra watches, and was not on the bridge during the critical time.

ISMAY. All true.

OFFICER. He was under company pressure, as were all captains, to get into port at the allotted time.

FIRST CLASS. Of course! Just "bang on" and hope for the best!

(ISMAY & OFFICER react. LIGHTS shift back to OLDER LIGHTOLLER and Interviewer.)

OLDER LIGHTOLLER. Maintaining course and speed in favorable weather and trusting the lookouts to sight ice in time was common practice of long standing. Captain Smith had done only that which other skilled men would have done in the same position. It is to be hoped that the last has been heard of this practice. What was a . . .

mistake in the case of the Titanic would without doubt be negligence in any similar case in the future.

(OLDER LIGHTOLLER & Interviewer exits. LIGHTS shift back.)

THIRD CLASS. But weather wasn't favorable, was it?

ISMAY and **OFFICER.** No.

FIRST CLASS. Then that should be Captain Smith's true legacy. Instead, both Inquiries found him virtually blameless and he was immortalized in bronze in Litchfield, England.

(SLIDE of CAPTAIN SMITH statue.)

ISMAY. Everything was against us that night.

OFFICER. We all–

FIRST CLASS. *(Interrupting.)* Did everything that was possible. As you have said. So somehow, there was absolutely no one at fault for this disaster.

OFFICER. If you wish to point a finger, madam, then I would suggest–

FIRST CLASS. Stanley Lord, of the Californian?

OFFICER. Oh yes, Captain Lord–whose crew had seen no less than eight rockets fired, reported it to their Captain three separate times, and did nothing!

ISMAY. They did try signaling with the Morse lamp.

OFFICER. They were nineteen miles away!

FIRST CLASS. Some say less than ten miles.

OFFICER. And worse, Lord didn't bother to wake their wireless operator!

ISMAY. They were right in the heart of the ice field–

OFFICER. Not an acceptable reason for inaction.

FIRST CLASS. Agreed.

ISMAY. I am not attempting to defend or condemn him—

OFFICER. His officers just stood and watched the rockets being fired; having received no orders to do otherwise.

FIRST CLASS. And so, the lights seen in the distance by the Titanic, were to be only a glimmer of false hope.

THIRD CLASS. Some of us saw more than just distant lights!

*(LIGHTS isolate **EVA HART**.)*

EVA HART. It wasn't just lights on the horizon, I saw a ship that was close by. Now, I of course cannot say that it was the Californian, but you could see it was a ship. And I saw our rockets being fired, which that ship must have seen.

(Exits.)

(LIGHTS shift back.)

THIRD CLASS. Many people saw that ship and couldn't believe she did nothing to help.

OFFICER. We even ordered some of the lifeboats to row towards it. Thinking they could reach her and come back for more passengers.

FIRST CLASS. So the Inquiries, the British one especially, found their scapegoat.

ISMAY. A burden he was to carry for the rest of his life.

FIRST CLASS. Though he continued to plead his case that the ship his crew saw was not the Titanic.

OFFICER. Yes, the "mystery ship" that also just happened to fire off rockets that night.

THIRD CLASS. A scapegoat does not help the hundreds of families who lost their providers!

ISMAY. No.

THIRD CLASS. And since neither Inquiry found White Star Line at fault, survivors were left with the Limited Liability Act.

FIRST CLASS. Another owner-friendly law. As the ship was now owned by J. P. Morgan, the American formula applied, making White Star liable for only $97,000.

THIRD CLASS. A ridiculously low amount of money!

ISMAY. At that point, I was powerless. The company would not listen to me.

FIRST CLASS. Then came a civil suit. And after four years of legal battles, finally another settlement with your company was made.

ISMAY. By 1913, it was no longer my company–

FIRST CLASS. White Star Line agreed to pay a lump sum of $664,000–

THIRD CLASS. But in return, the several hundred claimants had to drop all suits in both countries, and agree that White Star Line had "no knowledge of any negligence on the Titanic."

ISMAY. Yes . . .

THIRD CLASS. As always, most of the money went to the wealthy. The "steerage" averaged only $1,000 each from the settlement; but the rich? They received abundantly more. Renee Harris got $50,000!

FIRST CLASS. Her husband had run a successful theatre and–

THIRD CLASS. And?

FIRST CLASS. And she needed–

THIRD CLASS. Needed!?

(Pause.)

FIRST CLASS. Perhaps $50,000 was a bit unfair to the others.

THIRD CLASS. It was robbery!

(Pause.)

FIRST CLASS. Well, there was also the Titanic Relief Fund.

THIRD CLASS. Thank God for that! At least someone cared for the "steerage." Without that fund many would not have made it.

(Pause.)

FIRST CLASS. I understand that you even paid for a gravestone for crewman Ernest Freeman and supported his family for several years.

ISMAY. That is true. I will also reveal that I contributed ten thousand pounds towards the pension fund for widows of seamen on the Titanic and twenty five thousand pounds to help inaugurate the National Mercantile Marine fund.

FIRST CLASS. My, my.

ISMAY. It was important that the crew's families would have somewhere to turn.

FIRST CLASS. Quite admirable, Mr. Ismay.

ISMAY. Yes. Well. It was my . . . I did everything I could.

FIRST CLASS. Did you?

(Pause.)

ISMAY. I don't know anymore . . .

THIRD CLASS. *(Pointedly to ISMAY.)* Everyone did what they could. But the frightful memories never ceased . . .

(Various individual pools of LIGHT come up on RUTH BECKER, MARIE JERWAN, ERNEST ALLEN, EVA HART, FRANK PRENTICE just prior to each one entering. As they speak they stare at ISMAY. ISMAY returns to the same place he was at the beginning of Act One.)

RUTH BECKER. My mother's personality changed dramatically after the disaster. She was far more nervous and was given to emotional outbursts. For the rest of her life, she was never able to discuss the disaster without dissolving into tears.

M. JERWAN. For weeks after the tragedy I continually suffered from panic attacks and nightmares.

E. ALLEN. I'm still haunted by the sound of that girl struggling in the water. But what could I do? It was everyone for themselves.

EVA HART. I still have a vivid recollection of being absolutely petrified on that dark night with a sinking ship and people screaming.

F. PRENTICE. Few precautions. Not enough lifeboats. It was almost like murder wasn't it?

(LIGHTS dim. The rest of the ENSEMBLE slowly enters during the below and stare at ISMAY. SLIDE of CAPTAIN SMITH with the caption "Captain Smith in

*1907". MUSIC lightly underscores. During the below speech, each **ENSEMBLE** member speaks the names of several people who were lost in the disaster.)*

CAPTAIN SMITH. *(VOICE OVER.)* Shipbuilding is such a perfect art nowadays that absolute disaster, involving the passengers, is inconceivable. Whatever happens, there will be time enough before the vessel sinks to save the life of every person on board. I will go a bit further. I will say that I cannot imagine any condition that would cause the vessel to founder. Modern shipbuilding has gone beyond that. When anyone asks me how I can best describe my experience of nearly forty years at sea I merely say uneventful. In all my experiences I have never been in an accident worth speaking of . . .

CURTAIN

END OF ACT ONE

ACT TWO

SETTING:

Same as Act One.

AT RISE:

> *(The Act begins in total darkness. Several **ENSEMBLE** members are onstage. **ISMAY** sits alone in the dark. In the darkness we hear SFX–Wind Sounds and then Three Bells.)*

OFFICER. *(VOICE OVER, telephone sound.)* What do you see?

FLEET *(Live.)* Iceberg right ahead!

OFFICER. *(VOICE OVER, telephone sound.)* Thank you.

> *(LIGHTS come up dimly isolating **ISMAY**. The **ENSEMBLE** remains in darkness. **ISMAY**–as in the beginning of the Act One–looks old and upset. During the below, we hear SFX–Ship Scraping on Ice Sounds. Dialogue below overlaps slightly.)*

F.CLENCH. I was awakened by the crunching and jarring.

MRS. WHITE. It was as though we went over about a thousand marbles.

F. FLEET. It was just a slight grinding noise.

ISMAY. No. No . . . I can't . . .

> *(**ISMAY** becomes more agitated. **ENSEMBLE** voices become soft. The below left lines **underscore** the VOICE OVERS. SLIDES–**MR. MURDOCH** and **CAPTAIN SMITH**.)*

65

EVA HART. We felt a slight bump–just like a train pulling into a station, it just jerked.

MR. G. CROWE. I thought one of the propellers had been broken.

MRS. G.A.HARDER. It was a rumbling scraping noise.

C.E.H. STENGEL. I heard a slight crash.

MAJOR PEUCHEN. It was as though a heavy wave had struck our ship.

(ALL VOICE OVERS.)

CAPTAIN SMITH. Mr. Murdoch, what was that?

MR. MURDOCH. An iceberg, sir. I hard-a-starboarded and reversed the engines, but she was too close. I couldn't do any more.

CAPTAIN SMITH. Close the emergency doors.

MR. MURDOCH. The doors are already closed,sir.

ISMAY. No! I will not live through this again.

*(LIGHTS expand slightly as **FIRST CLASS, THIRD CLASS** and **OFFICER** come into **ISMAY'S** pool of light. **ENSEMBLE** exits looking at **ISMAY**.)*

FIRST CLASS. But the memories live on despite your wishes.

THIRD CLASS. Do you think you are the only one who continues to suffer?

ISMAY. Of course not. What an absurd question.

FIRST CLASS. And yet how little you know.

THIRD CLASS. Attention must be paid. Voices must be heard.

ISMAY. I will not! I simply can not endure it.

*(**ISMAY** pulls away slightly.)*

FIRST CLASS. You shall bear witness, Mr. Ismay.

(FIRST CLASS puts a hand on ISMAY'S shoulder. ISMAY feels strangely comforted.)

THIRD CLASS. A lifetime of events occurred that fateful evening.

OFFICER. It took only thirty seven seconds between receiving the call and the collision.

FIRST CLASS. Most of us sensed no danger at all.

(LIGHTS shift. SELENA COOK enters.)

S. COOK. "Oh, don't those boys make a noise" I said to my husband when I was awakened by the collision. You see, I assumed the boys were once again in the throws of a pillow fight.

(As she exits, she looks at ISMAY.)

(LIGHTS shift.)

FIRST CLASS. You awoke with a start, didn't you?

ISMAY. Yes. I knew the ship had struck something.

OFFICER. The poor men in the boiler rooms knew at once our situation was grave.

(LIGHTS shift. FRED BARRETT enters.)

F. BARRETT. The Second Engineer and I were talking together when the warning bell sounded. I got out a quick shout to warn everyone when came this ear shattering crash and the sea come rushing in. We just managed to dive through the watertight door as it slammed down. But that did little good as we were hit by another fat jet of sea water bursting into that room as well.

(As he exits, he looks at ISMAY.)

(LIGHTS shift.)

OFFICER. The bridge scrambled to assess the situation.

ISMAY. I could not believe it. I asked officer after officer—

OFFICER. But you heard from Thomas Andrews, the ship's designer, that it was a mathematical certainty. . .

ISMAY. The great ship was going to founder.

THIRD CLASS. In the bowels of your "great ship" the "steerage" already knew.

*(LIGHTS shift. **DANIEL BUCKLEY** enters.)*

D. BUCKLEY. I heard some terrible grating noise, and I jumped out on the floor, and the first thing I knew my feet were getting wet. I told the other fellows to get up, that there was something wrong and that water was coming in.

*(Off-stage laughter from a few **MEN** is heard.)*

MAN. *(Off Stage.)* Get back into bed, Daniel. You are not in Ireland now.

D. BUCKLEY. I got on my clothes as quick as I could and got out of the room. I did not see them any more after leaving our room.

*(Exits looking at **ISMAY**.)*

(LIGHTS shift.)

OFFICER. It took a full twenty-five minutes after the collision before the order was given to muster up the passengers and prepare the lifeboats.

FIRST CLASS. Twenty-five minutes . . .

ISMAY. Fortunately, only a handful of people knew the seriousness of the situation.

THIRD CLASS. Fortunately?

OFFICER. The captain did not want a panic on his hands.

ISMAY. The truth was a curse. Knowing there were lifeboat accommodations for less than half on board.

THIRD CLASS. The wealthy half.

FIRST CLASS. Everything was so haphazard. So many people were misinformed.

THIRD CLASS. Or not informed at all!

OFFICER. We had no general alarm, no PA systems, no sirens, nothing.

FIRST CLASS. Once again this "technological triumph" fails to impress.

(OFFICER & ISMAY react.)

THIRD CLASS. So, word of mouth ruled the evening.

FIRST CLASS. The first class stewards walked around, knocked on our doors, and tried to convince us there was a problem.

OFFICER. Which many of you refused to believe.

FIRST CLASS. I'll grant you that. In second class it was more a pounding on doors.

THIRD CLASS. And for the "steerage", they just threw open our doors and screamed at us.

ISMAY. It seems unlikely our stewards–

THIRD CLASS. It happened!

FIRST CLASS. For all of us, it became a quest for information.

(LIGHTS isolate MRS. DOUGLAS.)

MRS. DOUGLAS. I waited, but we received no orders; no one knocked at our door; we saw no officers nor stewards. Soon I heard from some one that the order had been given to put lifebelts on. I took three from our cabin, gave one to the maid, and told her to get off in the small boat when her turn came. My husband met me and asked, jestingly, "Mahala, what are you doing with those life preservers?

*(LIGHTS isolate **D. BUCKLEY**. **MRS. DOUGLAS** exits.)*

D. BUCKLEY. As I was walking two sailors came along, and were shouting: "All up on deck unless you want to get drowned."

THIRD CLASS. They never would have said that to a first class passenger.

*(LIGHTS isolate **MRS. RYERSON & EVA HART** talking together. **D. BUCKLEY** exits.)*

MRS. RYERSON. My steward told me, "Ms. Ryerson, there is talk of an iceberg, ma'am, and they have stopped, not to run into it." My husband remained quite calm. I however was paralyzed with fear.

*(LIGHTS isolate **HENRY ETCHES** talking with an **ENSEMBLE** member. **MRS. RYERSON & EVA HART** freeze.)*

H. ETCHES. I found No.78 cabin door still shut, and I banged with both hands on the door loudly.

(He moves to another pool of LIGHT and knocks.)

LADY. *(Off-Stage.)* What is it? Tell me what the trouble is.

H. ETCHES. It is necessary that you should open the door, and I will explain everything, but please put the life belts on or bring them in the corridor.

LADY. *(Off-Stage.)* Mr. Etches, I want to know what is the matter.

H. ETCHES. Kindly open the door.

*(Bangs again, then he moves back to the **ENSEMBLE** member.)*

Finally, I passed along. I never did see that door opened.

*(LIGHTS back to **MRS. RYERSON & EVA HART** talking together. **H. ETCHES** exits with the **ENSEMBLE** member he was talking with.)*

EVA HART. My mother literally pulled father out of bed and made him go up. My father came back very quickly. He picked me up and wrapped this blanket tightly around me as if I were a baby. My mother said nothing to him. And I used to say to her sometimes years afterwards "I can't understand why you didn't say to him 'what was it.'" And she said "I didn't have to, Eva. I didn't know what it was, but I knew it was this dreadful something that I would have to live with."

(They exit.)

*(LIGHTS isolate **COLONEL GRACIE** and **EDITH RUSSELL** talking together.)*

COLONEL GRACIE. I did not like the sound of the commotion, so I partially dressed myself, and went on deck. At that time I joined my friend, Mr. Clint Smith–Clinch–and he and I agreed to stick by each other through thick and thin if anything occurred.

E. RUSSELL. We were told we were only going to leave because it was rules and regulations, no danger whatsoever. We'd all be back for breakfast. Oh, Colonel Gracie, I thought it was perfectly asinine to leave a warm, comfortable ship to come back for breakfast. The English have got rules and regulations, but they're just plumb crazy. I was sticking to this ship, so I went to bed.

(E. RUSSELL goes to another pool of light.)

STEWARD. *(Off-Stage, knocking.)* Miss Russell, get up.

(Enters.) They're claiming that women and children should leave the ship.

E. RUSSELL. Well, then, please take the time to pack every trunk and suitcase, young man. Oh, and will you please guide my trunks through customs?

STEWARD. You go on and kiss your trunks goodbye.

(Exits.)

(E. RUSSELL goes back to COLONEL GRACIE.)

E. RUSSELL. I then sensed that the situation was perhaps, worse than I expected. So, I grabbed my lucky pig music box, and made my way to the boatdeck.

(LIGHTS expand on stage. COLONEL GRACIE and E. RUSSELL exit together. OLAUS ABELSETH enters while the OFFICER is crossing to speak to a STEWARD.)

O. ABELSETH. I saw one of the officers and I said to him: "Is there any danger?"

OFFICER. No. No . . .

(OFFICER rushes over to talk to STEWARD.)

O. ABELSETH. I was not satisfied with that, however, so I went down and told my brother-in-law and cousin, who were in the same compartment there.

(STEWARD and OFFICER part and start to exit. O. ABELSETH stops the STEWARD.)

O. ABELSETH. A little while later there was one of the stewards who came—

STEWARD. Be quiet, there is a ship coming!

(Exits.)

O. ABELSETH. That is all he said.

(Exits.)

(HELEN CANDEE enters with HUGH WOOLNER.)

H. CANDEE. Four of "our coterie"—Colonel Gracie's name for our little group—were playing bridge in the smoking room on A deck when suddenly there came a heavy grinding sort of a shock. Mr. Woolner and Mr. Steffanson came below to check on me in my stateroom. Naturally I was quite puzzled but otherwise all right.

H. WOOLNER. We then went for a walk and found the ship had a pronounced list to starboard. I could see Mrs. Candee was troubled, so I made a few jokes to improve her spirits.

H. CANDEE. Then, a cheerful young man suddenly appeared and handed me a small chunk of ice. It was so cold—And dear Mr. Woolner caressed my hand in an effort to warm it.

(LIGHTS shift, H. CANDEE & H. WOOLNER exit.)

FIRST CLASS. When we all were on deck, everyone was so quiet and self-possessed. Just standing there with our lifebelts on . . .

ISMAY. While I was dying on the inside.

FIRST CLASS. Interesting. You might not believe it, but my chief thought, and that of everyone else was not to make a fuss and to do as we were told.

(ISMAY reacts. LIGHTS shift. COLONEL GRACIE and E. RUSSELL enter talking.)

COLONEL GRACIE. I saw Mr. Clarence Moore and Major Archie Butt and Mr. Millet at about 1 o'clock and they were perfectly imperturbable, showing their confidence in the ship, that no disaster was going to take place.

(Exits with E. RUSSELL.)

(H. CANDEE & H. WOOLNER enter.)

H. CANDEE. On the stairs I met Edward Kent, another "coterie" member, and on impulse handed him a small ivory miniature of my mother, asking him to keep it for me. He was reluctant, having doubts about his own safety, but slipped it into his pocket. It was still there when his body was picked up a week later.

(Exits with H. WOOLNER.)

(NORMAN CHAMBERS enters talking with C.E.H. STENGEL.)

N. CHAMBERS. I was able to look directly into the trunk room, which was then filled with water. We were standing there joking about our baggage being completely soaked and about the letters which were floating about on top of the water. I personally felt no sense of danger, as this water was forward of the bulkhead. Wouldn't you agree, Mr. Stengel?

C.E.H. STENGEL. I think the officers were very cool, Mr. Chambers. They calmed the passengers by making them believe it was not a serious accident.

(They both exit.)

(LIGHTS shift.)

OFFICER. *(to FIRST CLASS.)* There you have it. Had we reported the true damage, very few passengers would have survived.

FIRST CLASS. What?

OFFICER. Everyone would have panicked, including the crew. No one would have had a fair chance.

FIRST CLASS. You truly believe that?

ISMAY. The will to survive is quite strong . . .

THIRD CLASS. At least you were given an opportunity to live! I guess this "fair chance" did not apply to the "steerage."

(LIGHTS shift. D. BUCKLEY enters.)

D. BUCKLEY. They tried to keep us down at first on our steerage deck. They did not want us to go up to the first-class place at all. Some tried to get out. There was one steerage passenger getting up the steps, and just as he was going in a little gate a sailor came along and chucked him down. Then this sailor locked the gate. This fellow got excited, went up after him, broke the lock on it, and ran after the sailor that threw him down.

(Exits.)

THIRD CLASS. Are you listening? Gates were locked and crewmen, drunk with power, kept us down below.

*(LIGHTS shift. **ISMAY** watches intently. **O. ABELSETH** enters.)*

O. ABELSETH. We waited there on the deck a long while until one of the officers came and hollered for all of the ladies to come up on the boat deck. The gate was opened and these two girls went up. We stayed a little while longer, and then they said, "Everybody." We went up and over to the port side of the ship, and there were just one or two boats that were left.

(Exits.)

OFFICER. There were difficulties communicating with the steerage. So many were foreigners—

THIRD CLASS. That does not excuse locked gates! People could have been led up on deck—

OFFICER. But so many of them insisted on bringing their luggage—

THIRD CLASS. Their only possessions in the world!

*(**OFFICER** crosses away, is blocked by **RENEE HARRIS** entering. **ISMAY** reacts and becomes more anguished during the below.)*

R. HARRIS. There was this extremely rude man laughing at the third class passengers who were milling around toting everything they owned in trunks and suitcases.

*(**OFFICER** crosses away, is blocked by **O. ABELSETH** entering.)*

O. ABELSETH. There were a lot of steerage people there that were crawling along one of these cranes that they had on deck, over the railing, and away up to the boat deck. They could not get up there any other way because this gate was shut.

*(OFFICER crosses away and is blocked by **THIRD CLASS**.)*

THIRD CLASS. Most "steerage" passengers weren't lucky enough to make it to the boat deck in time, if at all. Some tried to navigate the back ways through the endless passageways and decks. But even then, we found trouble.

*(**KATIE GILNAGH** enters on the other side of the **OFFICER**.)*

K. GILNAGH. We had finally made our way up to the second class gate and found it was locked and guarded. My friend Jim Farrell had to do some heavy convincing before they'd open it up and let us ladies through. But they finally did, and I never saw dear Jimmy again.

*(**O. ABELSETH, K. GILNAGH, R. HARRIS,** and **THIRD CLASS** converge on the **OFFICER** and **ISMAY**.)*

THIRD CLASS. Only 25% of the third class was saved. But the first class saw 63% of their members survive!

*(**OFFICER** and **ISMAY** react. LIGHTS dim. MUSIC bridge. **O. ABELSETH, K. GILNAGH, R. HARRIS** exit. LIGHTS shift. .)*

FIRST CLASS. Tell me, when was the order finally given to start loading women and children into the lifeboats?

OFFICER. 12:30am . . .

FIRST CLASS. Fifty minutes after the impact!

OFFICER. Yes . . . Even then, passengers still had a distinct lack of concern.

*(LIGHTS shift to Hearing. **S. SMITH** is questioning **MRS. WHITE** and **LIGHTOLLER**.)*

S. SMITH. Mrs. White, please tell us what you did after the impact.

MRS. WHITE. There was nothing terrifying about it at all. We went right up on deck ourselves and found everyone simply standing around. It seemed all we did was wait. Clearly no one knew what they were doing.

S. SMITH. Where did you enter your lifeboat?

MRS. WHITE. I entered the lifeboat from the top deck, where the boats were. There was no other deck to the steamer except the top deck. It was a perfect rat trap.

S. SMITH. Thank you, Mrs. White. Mr. Lightoller, were there always people ready to go?

LIGHTOLLER. Perfectly quiet and ready.

S. SMITH. Any jostling, pushing, or crowding?

LIGHTOLLER. No sir. They could not have stood quieter if they had been in church. In fact, with the last couple of boats, it was difficult to find women to fill them.

*(LIGHTS shift. **LIGHTOLLER, S. SMITH** and **MRS. WHITE** exit.)*

OFFICER. Despite the passenger's early casual attitude, we all worked diligently to load the women and children into the lifeboats.

FIRST CLASS. Sometimes by force.

OFFICER. If necessary.

*(ISMAY reacts. LIGHTS isolate **HELEN BISHOP**.)*

H. BISHOP. I had no idea that it was time to get off, but the officer took my arm and told me to be very quiet and get in immediately. Then my husband and I were pushed in and we were lowered away with 28 people, of which were only thirteen passengers. Among those were several unmarried men, I noticed, and three or four foreigners.

THIRD CLASS. Foreigners–another word for the "steerage".

*(LIGHTS isolate **MOLLY BROWN**.)*

MOLLY BROWN. Look, all I wanted was to get all these young girls off the ship. I wasn't thinking much about myself. Everyone was acting like it was some sort of "minor inconvenience", but I had heard better. Matter of fact, I probably wouldn't be here today if two sailors hadn't picked me up and tossed me in a lifeboat.

*(LIGHTS isolate **F. EVANS**.)*

F. EVANS. The first child was passed over, and I caught it by the dress. It was dangling. I had to swing it, and a woman caught it. That was the only accident, except this woman. She seemed a bit nervous. She did not like to jump, at first, and when she did jump, she didn't go far enough, and she went between the ship and the boat. Her boot caught on the rail on the next deck and she was pulled in by some men underneath.

*(LIGHTS shift to a dim general wash of the stage. **ENSEMBLE** members are slowly being loaded into Lifeboats. **H. CANDEE** enters escorted by **H. WOOLNER** and an **ENSEMBLE** member to a Lifeboat being loaded on Stage Left by **LIGHTOLLER**. and **CREW MEMBER 1**. On Stage Right is the **OFFICER** and **CREW MEMBER 2**. After a few moments of Lifeboat loading, LIGHTS slowly isolate the **OFFICER'S** Lifeboat area.)*

*(Note 1: Whenever the Lifeboats are "full", the attending Officer waves both of his arms as if ordering to "lower away". **ENSEMBLE** members in the boat then solemnly stand up and slowly exit.*

*(Note 2: **LIGHTOLLER** allows only women and children into his boat. **OFFICER** allows some men into his.)*

H. CANDEE. Mr. Woolner and Mr. Steffanson hurried me into Boat 6. Colonel Gracie was quite busy elsewhere, having offered his services to four other "unprotected ladies" and doing his best to see them all into the boats. Three of "our coterie" died on the Titanic. I couldn't bear . . . I wasn't able to see the other two survivors again.

*(**E. RUSSELL** enters and makes her way to the Lifeboat being loaded by the **OFFICER**. **H. WOOLNER** exits.)*

E. RUSSELL. I was wearing the only warm woolen dress I had, a sheath dress so tight that from my hips to my ankles I was practically . . . well, I would say I was in a potato sack. I couldn't walk. I had to hobble. I couldn't be dressed more ridiculously.

OFFICER. Come on Miss Russell, you've got to get off this ship.

E. RUSSELL. Not me. How do you expect me to get off anything with this thing I've got on? I'm a prisoner in my own skirt. I can't even walk much less jump across the ocean into a lifeboat!

CREW MEMBER 2. If you don't want to go, we'll save your baby anyway!

(Takes wrapped bundle & throws into a Lifeboat.)

E. RUSSELL. My lucky pig!

(OFFICER and CREW MEMBER 2 pick her up and toss her into Lifeboat.)

E. RUSSELL. I fell into the bottom of the boat. I quickly scrounged around and found the pig. The poor thing had no nose and two broken legs! Fortunately, it still played its little song, "La Maxixe". It later helped to calm the poor children who were in the boat with me.

*(LIGHTS isolate **C.E.H.STENGEL** far upstage. **ENSEMBLE freezes**.)*

C.E.H. STENGEL. There was a small emergency boat near the bow in which there were Sir Duff Gordon and his wife and Miss Francatelli.

(SLIDE–MR. MURDOCH.)

Could I get into that boat? There is no one else around.

MR. MURDOCH. *(VOICE OVER.)* All right. Jump in.

C.E.H. STENGEL. The railing was rather high and I attempted to jump in. But I ended up ungracefully rolling onto the bottom of the boat.

(He walks out of the light and is unseen as we hear him fall and yell.)

MR. MURDOCH. *(VOICE OVER. Laughing.)* That is the funniest sight I have seen tonight.

(LIGHTS shift.)

THIRD CLASS. That boat left with only twelve people on board!

FIRST CLASS. When it could have carried forty . . .

*(LIGHTS isolate **ALFRED CRAWFORD**. **ENSEMBLE un-freezes** but moves in **slow motion**. SLIDES–MRS. IDA STRAUS & MR. ISIDOR STRAUS.)*

A. CRAWFORD. Mrs. Isidor Straus and her husband were there at boat number eight. We filled that boat up with women first and Mrs. Straus had placed her maid in the boat and handed her a rug. She made an attempt to get in then stepped back and clung to her husband.

MRS. STRAUSS. *(VOICE OVER.)* We have been together all these years. Where you go I go.

A. CRAWFORD. I tried to get her in to the lifeboat and she refused altogether to leave Mr. Straus. The second time we went up to Mr. Straus, and said "I am sure nobody would object to an old gentleman like you getting in. There seems to be room in this boat."

MR. STRAUSS. *(VOICE OVER.)* I will not go before the other men.

A. CRAWFORD. And so they were left behind.

(ENSEMBLE freezes. LIGHTS isolate EVA HART who is already in the OFFICER'S Lifeboat. A. CRAWFORD exits.)

EVA HART. My father put me into the boat and told me "Eva, be good and hold Mommy's hand". I thought he was coming after me, but he didn't. Then it dawned on me of course that he wasn't coming, that I wouldn't see him anymore.

(LIGHTS go to a dim general wash. ENSEMBLE unfreezes and moves at normal speed. LIGHTOLLER'S Lifeboat should be "full" at this point, so LIGHTOLLER gives the signal to "lower away". The ENSEMBLE in that boat then exits. LIGHTS slowly isolate the area near LIGHTOLLER'S Lifeboat and MAJOR PEUCHEN is nearby.)

MAJOR PEUCHEN. As one boat was being lowered, about halfway down, the Quartermaster in it called out—

QUARTERMASTER. *(Off Stage.)* We will have to have some more seamen here! There's only one in the lifeboat.

LIGHTOLLER. I only have two up here and I need them for other boats.

MAJOR PEUCHEN. Mr. Lightoller, Major Peuchen. I will go, if you like.

LIGHTOLLER. Are you a seaman?

MAJOR PEUCHEN. I am a yachtsman.

LIGHTOLLER. If you are sailor enough to get out on that fall you can go down.

*(LIGHTS narrow to isolating **LIGHTOLLER** only. **MAJOR PEUCHEN** exits. **ENSEMBLE** freezes.)*

LIGHTOLLER. It was a difficult rope to get to, over the ship's side, 8 feet away, and taking a long swing on a dark night. But he proved a sailor by making it all the way down.

*(BLACKOUT. MUSIC bridge. **MR. LOWE** enters and goes to the Stage Right Lifeboat. LIGHTS slowly come up isolating **OFFICER, ISMAY, FIRST CLASS** and **THIRD CLASS, ENSEMBLE** are frozen.)*

OFFICER. Loading the lifeboats was grueling work. Even though it was freezing, we were all sweating profusely.

ISMAY. I did everything in my power to convince people to get into the boats.

*(LIGHTS isolate **ISMAY-1912** near the Stage Right Lifeboat with **MR. LOWE. ENSEMBLE** un-freezes moves at **normal speed**.)*

ISMAY–1912. Lower away! Lower away! Lower away! Lower away!

MR. LOWE. If you will get to hell out of that I shall be able to do something. Do you want me to lower away quickly? You will have me drown the whole lot of them.

*(ISMAY-1912 exits. LIGHTS shift back to **OFFICER**, **ISMAY**, **FIRST CLASS** and **THIRD CLASS**. ENSEMBLE freezes.)*

ISMAY. I said very little after that. I simply continued to assist in loading.

FIRST CLASS. One of your better choices. You kept to the starboard side of the ship, correct?

ISMAY. I did. Why–

FIRST CLASS. Because if you were a man, your chances of survival depended on what side of the ship you were on.

OFFICER. On the starboard side Officer Murdoch simply wanted to fill the boats. So when women were not around, he would allow men on board. Officer Lightoller on the port side, misinterpreted the order, "women and children first" to mean "women and children only".

FIRST CLASS. But this didn't stop some men from trying.

*(LIGHTS isolate **MRS. DOUGLAS** in the Stage Left Lifeboat. **ENSEMBLE un-freezes** and moves in **slow motion**.)*

MRS. DOUGLAS. Mr. Boxhall was trying to get our boat off, and just before we got in, the Captain called from a megaphone–

(SLIDE–CAPTAIN SMITH.)

CAPTAIN SMITH. *(VOICE OVER. Old megaphone sound.)* How many of the crew are in that boat? Get out of there, every man of you!

MRS. DOUGLAS. And I could see a solid row of men, from bow to stern, crawl over on to the deck. Several women then got in.

(LIGHTS shift back.)

OFFICER. *(to FIRST CLASS.)* That doesn't sound like a "man in a daze".

*(LIGHTS isolate **D. BUCKLEY** near the Stage Right Lifeboat. **ENSEMBLE** moves at **normal speed**.)*

D. BUCKLEY. When the sixth lifeboat was prepared, there was a big crowd of men standing on the deck. And they all jumped in so I said I would take my chance with them. So I went into the boat.

(Crawls into one of the Lifeboats.)

Two officers came along and said all the men should get out and let the ladies in. The men at first fought and would not get out. But the officer drew their revolvers and fired shots over our heads,

(SFX gunshots.)

and all but six men got out. I think they were firemen and sailors. I was crying. A woman who was in the boat threw her shawl over me and told me to stay in there.

(Throws a shawl over his head.)

They did not see me, and the boat was lowered down into the water.

*(LIGHTS expand. **H. WOOLNER** enters.)*

H. WOOLNER. We saw these two flashes of the pistol, and Steffanson and I went up to help clear that boat of the men who were climbing in. I think they were probably third-class passengers.

(H. WOOLNER exits.)

THIRD CLASS. Of course! All the troublemakers were "steerage".

FIRST CLASS. I'm sure most of the men would have rushed the boats had they truly known their fate.

THIRD CLASS. Hugh Woolner himself jumped into a lifeboat being lowered!

(Stage Left & Right Lifeboats should be full at this point. ***OFFICER & LIGHTOLLER*** *give the order to lower away. After a few seconds those* ***ENSEMBLE*** *members exit. More* ***ENSEMBLE*** *members enter and go towards the Lifeboats. LIGHTS slowly isolate the Stage Left Lifeboat area.* ***MRS. WHITE*** *gets into the Lifeboat.)*

MRS. WHITE. They speak of the bravery of the men. I do not think there was any particular bravery, because none of the men thought it was going down. If they had thought the ship was going down, they would not have frivoled as they did about it.

(Two ***MALE ENSEMBLE*** *members cross the stage.)*

MAN. When you come back you will need a pass, Mrs. White!

ANOTHER MAN. You cannot get on tomorrow morning without a pass!

MRS. WHITE. They never would have said these things if anybody had had any idea that the ship was going to sink.

(BLACKOUT. MUSIC bridge. SLIDE–MR. GUGGEN-HEIM. During the VOICE OVER, the ENSEMBLE continues pantomiming being loaded into Lifeboats moving in slow motion.)

MR. GUGGENHEIM. *(VOICE OVER.)* We have dressed up in our best and are prepared to go down like gentlemen. Please tell my wife that I've done my best at doing my duty.

(LIGHTS isolate OFFICER, ISMAY, FIRST CLASS and THIRD CLASS. ENSEMBLE freezes.)

ISMAY. Like gentlemen . . . Duty . . .

OFFICER. It was not until the list became quite pronounced and the bow was near water level, that people began to take the situation seriously.

(LIGHTS expand. ENSEMBLE un-freezes and moves at normal speed. OFFICER crosses and joins CREW MEMBER 2 who is helping to load the Stage Right Lifeboat. MR. LOWE exits.)

FIRST CLASS. The anguish of families being parted was unbearable.

(After a few seconds of loading the Lifeboats, the LIGHTS narrow to the area around LIGHTOLLER'S Lifeboat. MRS. RYERSON, JACK RYERSON and MR. RYERSON are there.)

MRS. RYERSON. Please my darling, let me stay with you!

MR. RYERSON. Emily, you must obey orders. You must go when your turn comes. I'll stay with John Thayer. We will be all right. You take a boat going to New York.

(SFX–rocket being fired off.)

MRS. RYERSON. There are a circle of ships coming to rescue us?

MR. RYERSON. Yes. You hear the rockets going up? They're signals of distress.

MRS. RYERSON. Come along, Jack. Into the lifeboat.

LIGHTOLLER. That boy can't go.

MR. RYERSON. Of course, that boy goes with his mother; he is only 13!

LIGHTOLLER. Very well then. No more boys.

*(**LIGHTOLLER** helps **JACK RYERSON** into the Stage Left Lifeboat. **MRS. RYERSON** tearfully kisses **MR. RYERSON**. **LIGHTOLLER** helps her into the Lifeboat. When she is in the Lifeboat, LIGHTS isolate **MRS. RYERSON** and **JACK RYERSON**. This Stage Left Lifeboat should be full at this point. **LIGHTOLLER** gives the signal to lower away. **ENSEMBLE** freezes.)*

MRS. RYERSON. As we left, my husband and the other men I knew were all standing there together very quietly.

*(**ENSEMBLE un-freezes** and moves at **normal speed**. **ENSEMBLE** in the Stage Left Lifeboat exit. LIGHTS isolate the Stage Right Lifeboat. **MRS. BECKER** is near the Lifeboat. **RUTH BECKER** is also there but farther away. She watches for a moment.)*

RUTH BECKER. My three younger siblings were put into boat 11 and before Mother knew it, the order was given to lower away.

*(**OFFICER** gives the order to lower away.)*

Mother called out—

MRS. BECKER. Oh please let me go with my children!

*(**OFFICER** gestures and **MRS. BECKER** gets into the Lifeboat. **OFFICER** gestures again to lower away.)*

RUTH BECKER. She quickly realized that I was still on board the Titanic.

MRS. BECKER. Ruth, get into another boat!

*(**ENSEMBLE** in Stage Right Lifeboat exit. As **RUTH BECKER** speaks, she runs over to the Stage Left Lifeboat. LIGHTS shift to the **LIGHTOLLER** Stage Left Lifeboat area. **LIGHTOLLER** and **CREW MEMBER 1** pick her up and drop her in the boat during the below.)*

RUTH BECKER. I ran over to Boat 13 and Officer Lightoller picked me up and dropped me in the already full boat. I was too excited to feel afraid. I remember looking up to the decks above and I thought "What is to become of all these people?

*(LIGHTS shift to a dim general wash. There is a few seconds of loading Lifeboats. **RUTH BECKER'S** boat–Stage Left–is lowered away and the **ENSEMBLE** Members in it exit. When they do, **MR. GOLDSMITH**, **MR. THEOBALD**, **MRS. GOLDSMITH**, and **FRANKIE GOLDSMITH** enter and cross to the **LIGHTOLLER** Lifeboat area.)*

F. GOLDSMITH. Our friend, Mr. Theobald, took his marriage ring off his finger and gave it to mother.

MR. THEOBALD. *(Handing her a ring.)* Mrs. Goldsmith, if I don't make it to New York will you see that my wife gets this.

MRS. GOLDSMITH. Of course.

*(MR.GOLDSMITH puts his arm around **MRS. GOLDSMITH** and kisses her. He then puts his hands on **F. GOLDSMITH'S** shoulders.)*

MR. GOLDSMITH. So long Frankie, I'll see you later.

*(**MR. GOLDSMITH & MR. THEOBALD** exit. LIGHTS isolate **F. GOLDSMITH** and **MRS. GOLDSMITH**. ENSEMBLE freezes.)*

F. GOLDSMITH. I'll never forget climbing that steel ladder to the boatdeck and being rushed along. There was a human chain of seamen who were trying to prevent a rush on the lifeboat. One man broke through and went in front of my mother–

MRS. GOLDSMITH. But I just shoved him aside and said "If my husband can not come, then this nasty chap can't either!"

F. GOLDSMITH. The seamen gave her a hearty cheer as they moved us into the lifeboat. It never crossed my mind that I had seen my father for the last time.

*(**ENSEMBLE** un-freezes and **F. GOLDSMITH & MRS. GOLDSMITH** get into the Stage Left Lifeboat. LIGHTS slowly isolate **RHODA ABBOTT** in a small area. **ENSEMBLE** freezes. SLIDES of her two sons.)*

R. ABBOTT. Clasping my two teenaged sons' hands, we watched anxiously as women and children were being loaded. When finally our turn came my heart sank. I realized my precious boys would not be allowed on board. How they considered them to be "men" I will never know. So I stepped back and prayed another boat would save us all.

*(**R. ABBOTT** freezes. LIGHTS isolate **R. HARRIS**.)*

R. HARRIS. I've played out the scene in my head a thousand times. We were passing through the bridge where the Captain was standing with the little doctor. That was my name for him; he had nursed my broken arm. I had slipped on a teacake the day before! It was past 1:30 and the Captain looked amazed when he saw me.

*(SLIDES of **CAPTAIN SMITH** and **DR. W. F. N. O'LOUGHLIN**. LIGHTS isolating **R. HARRIS** shift to blue.)*

CAPTAIN SMITH. *(VOICE OVER.)* My God woman, why aren't you in a lifeboat?

R. HARRIS. I won't leave my husband. I won't leave my husband!

Dr. O'LOUGHLIN. *(VOICE OVER.)* Isn't Mrs. Harris a brick?

CAPTAIN SMITH. *(VOICE OVER.)* She's a little fool. She's handicapping her husband's chances to save himself.

R. HARRIS. Can he be saved if I go?

CAPTAIN SMITH. *(VOICE OVER.)* Yes. There are plenty of rafts in the stern and the men can make for them if you women give them a chance.

*(LIGHTS expand. **ENSEMBLE un-freezes** and moves at **normal speed**. **R. HARRIS** crosses to the **OFFICER'S** Lifeboat. LIGHTS narrow to the Stage Right Lifeboat area. The **OFFICER** and a **CREW MEMBER** pick up **R. HARRIS** and put her into the Lifeboat. SLIDE–**MR. H. B. HARRIS**.)*

R. HARRIS. I had no time to protest. I was picked up and I felt myself being tossed into the nowhere.

MR. H. B. HARRIS. *(VOICE OVER.)* Catch my wife. Be careful–she has a broken arm.

*(LIGHTS isolate **R. HARRIS** in the Lifeboat. **ENSEMBLE** freezes.)*

R. HARRIS. Those are the last words I ever heard my beloved Henry speak.

*(LIGHTS shift to a dim general light. **ENSEMBLE** unfreezes and moves at **normal speed**–this time more desperately. **R. ABBOTT** exits. **OFFICER** gives the order to lower away. **ENSEMBLE** in the Stage Right Lifeboat exit. **ISMAY-1912** enters and crosses to the **LIGHTOLLER** Lifeboat on Stage Left. Just as **LIGHTOLLER** gives the order to lower away, **ISMAY-1912** steps into it. **ISMAY** reacts. After a few seconds the **ENSEMBLE** in the Stage Left Lifeboat exit. Two Female **ENSEMBLE** members enter escorted by **COLONEL GRACIE.** They are helped in to the Stage Right Lifeboat by **COLONEL GRACIE,** where the **OFFICER** is working.)*

COLONEL GRACIE. The crew seemed to resent my working with them at first, but they were very glad when I worked with them later on. Every opportunity I had to help, I helped.

*(**CAROLINE BROWN** enters and **FIRST CLASS** goes to her. **COLONEL GRACIE** crosses to them.)*

C. BROWN. When the scene was becoming more panicky, we were being hurried from lifeboat to lifeboat, but each was filled with passengers.

COLONEL GRACIE. Come along, ladies.

(COLONEL GRACIE takes C. BROWN & FIRST CLASS to the Stage Right Lifeboat being loaded by the OFFICER.)

OFFICER. This boat is overcrowded. Find another.

LIGHTOLLER. *(calling out.)* There's room for one more!

COLONEL GRACIE. Hurry ladies. I'm guessing the ship has less than fifteen minutes left.

(COLONEL GRACIE grabs FIRST CLASS and C. BROWN by the arm and crosses over the Stage Left Lifeboat being loaded by LIGHTOLLER.)

C. BROWN. *(as they are approaching.)* There are places for both of us!

LIGHTOLLER. There's room for only one more woman.

C. BROWN. What?

FIRST CLASS. Go on, Caroline.

C. BROWN. No. We both can—

FIRST CLASS. You have children. Please, take this lady.

(FIRST CLASS pushes C. BROWN towards the boat.)

C. BROWN. Wait!

(LIGHTOLLER and CREW MEMBER 1 pick up C. BROWN and toss her into the Stage Left Lifeboat.)

C. BROWN. I couldn't take my eyes off of that sweet woman's face as we were lowered.

WOMAN. *(In the same lifeboat as C. BROWN. Shouting to FIRST CLASS.)* There's another boat going to be put down for you!

(LIGHTS shift, isolating FIRST CLASS. ENSEMBLE freezes.)

FIRST CLASS. But there was no other boat for me . . . The fortune teller had been right–beware the water . . .

*(Slow BLACKOUT. MUSIC bridge. **ALL ENSEMBLE** exits. LIGHTS slowly come back up, isolating **FIRST CLASS, ISMAY, THIRD CLASS** and **OFFICER**.)*

FIRST CLASS. *(to ISMAY.)* Things became worse towards the end.

ISMAY. That is correct, unfortunately.

THIRD CLASS. *(to OFFICER.)* Mr. Lightoller anticipated that, didn't he? When he took Chief Officer Wilde to where the firearms were stored–

OFFICER. He did. But–

THIRD CLASS. He handed Wilde a revolver and slipped one into his own pocket, "just in case".

OFFICER. We had to be prepared for anything.

THIRD CLASS. Prepared for the worst, you mean?

*(SFX–Ship Creaking. LIGHTS shift to far upstage. The entire **ENSEMBLE** is in a crowd, pushing and shoving, while some Officers and Crew Members block their way.)*

OFFICER. The crowd surging around the boats were getting unruly.

*(**THIRD CLASS** and **FIRST CLASS** go near to the **OFFICER**.)*

THIRD CLASS. And you and your fellow officers were yelling and cursing at men to stand back and let the women get into the boats.

*(**JACK THAYER** pushes his way through the Crowd. **ENSEMBLE** disperses being pushed by the Officers and Crew. LIGHTS isolate **JACK THAYER**.)*

J. THAYER. A large crowd of men was pressing to get into the two forward starboard boats. Two men dropped into the boat from the deck above. As they jumped, Purser McElroy fired twice in the air.

*(SFX two gun shots. **J. THAYER & ENSEMBLE** exits.)*

(LIGHTS shift.)

FIRST CLASS. Hugh Woolner thought it was Officer Murdoch.

*(LIGHTS isolate **COLONEL GRACIE.**)*

COLONEL GRACIE. Some of the steerage passengers tried to rush the boat, and Officer Lightoller fired off a pistol to make them get out, which they did.

*(LIGHTS shift back. **COLONEL GRACIE** exits.)*

THIRD CLASS. Discrimination at its finest. When in doubt, point a finger at the "steerage" passengers.

FIRST CLASS. None of us intend to be demeaning.

THIRD CLASS. No. You just paint a picture of the "lower classes" as being "unruly". Can you imagine what it feels like to be referred to as "steerage"?

FIRST CLASS. No. I can't . . .

THIRD CLASS. What if you were called something worse?

*(LIGHTS isolate **MR. LOWE.**)*

MR. LOWE. We were being lowered down the decks and I saw a lot of Italians, Latin people, all along the ship's rails–and they were all glaring, like wild beasts, ready to spring. That is why I yelled to look out, and let go, bang, right along the ship's side. I said "Anybody attempting to get into these boats while we are lowering them, I will shoot them."

(LIGHTS shift back. **MR. LOWE** *exits.)*

THIRD CLASS. Wild beasts!

FIRST CLASS. I . . . don't know what to say . . .

THIRD CLASS. I'm sure you don't!

(Turns towards the **OFFICER.***)*

And the officers didn't just fire in the air. Some of the "steerage" were victims—

OFFICER. That is outrageous!

THIRD CLASS. Is it? Karl Midtsjo.

(As **KARL MIDTSJO** *&* **EUGENE DALY** *enter,* **THIRD CLASS** *directs* **OFFICER** *towards them.)*

K. MIDTSJO. It's been four days since the disaster and I can still hear the cries for help. Some were shot when they wanted to crowd their way up into the boats

THIRD CLASS. Eugene Daly.

E. DALY. When a boat was being lowered an officer pointed a revolver and said "if any man tried to get in, he would shoot him on the spot." I saw the officer shoot two men dead because they tried to get in the boat.

OFFICER. That is merely hearsay—

THIRD CLASS. Hearsay?! Two separate accounts written shortly after the accident? With neither one knowing the other. Even one of your precious first class passengers, George Rhiems, put it into a letter.

*(***THIRD CLASS** *directs* **OFFICER** *towards* **GEORGE RHEIMS.***)*

G. RHEIMS. While the last boat was leaving, I saw an officer with a revolver fire a shot and kill a man who was trying to climb into it. As there remained nothing more for him to do, the officer told us, "Gentlemen, each man for himself, Good-bye." He gave a military salute and then fired a bullet into his head.

*(**K. MIDTSJO, E. DALY** and **G. RHEIMS** exit looking at the **OFFICER**. .)*

OFFICER. That never– That is completely untrue!

THIRD CLASS. Most likely it was officer Murdoch or Wilde.

OFFICER. They wouldn't have–

THIRD CLASS. Neither body was recovered, so I guess we'll never know. But your men did fire at us.

OFFICER. You are sadly mistaken!

THIRD CLASS. No! I–

ISMAY. For God's sake stop this!

(Pause.)

FIRST CLASS. What can be agreed upon is that things got unruly as the lifeboats became scarce.

ISMAY. Yes. . .

FIRST CLASS. And that's when you decided to leave, correct?

ISMAY. We've been through this before, madam.

FIRST CLASS. Oh? Simply couldn't find any other women anywhere?

ISMAY. No, madam, we could not.

FIRST CLASS. I find that difficult to–

ISMAY. Madam, before you begin your self-righteous probing of choices made, please listen carefully: for whatever reason, there was no throng of people pushing to get onto that lifeboat. So after repeated calling the decision was made to lower the boat–though several seats were open. Suddenly, a terrible choice lay before me–a small wooden boat that represented life and safety, or a slow lingering demise in frigid waters. Tell me madam, what would you have me do? With a wife, children, and a world that would be demanding answers, what moral, dignified and "gentlemanly" decision would you have me make?

(He waits a moment for an answer. When there is none he continues.)

When was it decided that certain death is a preferable choice when one has made a commitment to their family? Perhaps we should ask Mrs. Astor, or Mrs. Ryerson, or Mrs. Hays, how "comforted" they feel because their husbands "heroically stayed with the sinking ship".

(Pause.)

I find this whole attitude absurd and unnecessarily abusive.

FIRST CLASS. My apologies, Mr. Ismay.

ISMAY. Thank you.

(LIGHTS dim. MUSIC bridge.)

FIRST CLASS. *(to ISMAY.)* While your lifeboat escape was without incident, there were others who faced extreme challenges.

(LIGHTS isolate DAISY MINAHAN in a Lifeboat.)

D. MINAHAN. When we finally were being lowered we were at an angle of 45 degrees and expected to be thrown into the sea; which thankfully did not happen, somebody cut a line and we went on down fine.

*(LIGHTS isolate **RUTH BECKER** in a Lifeboat. **D. MINAHAN** exits. SFX–sounds described below.)*

RUTH BECKER. When we reached the sea a blast of exhaust water pushed our boat astern so that we found ourselves directly below boat Number 15, which was being lowered. The crew tried to release the ropes, but they were so taut the mechanisms would not work. Everyone started calling desperately to those on deck to stop lowering, but the crew either could not hear or ignored us.

*(**ENSEMBLE** calls in a panic from Off Stage. LIGHTS on **RUTH BECKER** narrow.)*

It came closer and closer, and several men began to press their hands against the bottom, trying push it away. Finally, two of the seaman cut the ropes constricting us and we drifted out from under No.15 just before it landed. We rowed away from the Titanic just as fast as we could.

*(LIGHTS isolate **MRS. RYERSON** in a Lifeboat. **RUTH BECKER** exits.)*

MRS. RYERSON. Presently we were lowered away. It was but a short distance to the water, and I then realized for the first time how far the ship had sunk. The deck we left was only about twenty feet from the sea–instead of its usual seventy feet. I could see all the portholes open and water washing in, and the decks still lighted. In a few minutes after several other men–not sailors–came down the ropes over the davits and dropped into our boat, the order was given to pull away. But there was a confusion of orders and no one seemed to know what to do.

*(LIGHTS shift back to **ISMAY, FIRST CLASS, THIRD CLASS** and **OFFICER. MRS. RYERSON** exits.)*

ISMAY. Such disorder. So many hardships . . .

FIRST CLASS. You shall continue to bear witness, Mr. Ismay. Bravery and unselfishness were also seen that night.

*(LIGHTS isolate **EDWINA TROUT.** SLIDES of her Daughters.)*

E. TROUT. I don't know his name. Nobody knows his name. My two little girls and I were trying to find our way up on deck.

*(**CREWMAN** comes running in.)*

CREWMAN. This way.

(She follows him to another part of the stage.)

E. TROUT. We don't have any lifebelts!

CREWMAN. Come with me to my cabin.

*(**CREWMAN** takes her to another part of the stage. He exits briefly. He re-enters, hands her a Lifebelt.)*

CREWMAN. There, Madam. If you're saved, please pray for me.

(He exits.)

E. TROUT. I passed on this supreme kindness when I was in the lifeboat. Before we were lowered, a third class passenger came forward with a baby in his arms.

(CHARLES THOMAS Enters and crosses to E. TROUT.)

C. THOMAS. Please! Help me save my three month old nephew!

(E. TROUT takes the baby from him.)

C. THOMAS. Thank you!

(They share a moment.)

W. E. TROUT. Edwina Troutt.

C. THOMAS. Charles Thomas.

(LIGHTS dim. E. TROUT and C. THOMAS exit. Short MUSIC bridge. LIGHTS shift, isolating O. ABELSETH and CHARLES JOUGHIN talking together.)

O. ABELSETH. One of the officers came up and said as he walked by, "Are there any sailors here?" I did not say anything even though I had been a fishing man for six years. I would have gone, Charles, but my brother-in-law and my cousin said, in the Norwegian language: "Let us stay here together."

C. JOUGHIN. I sent all 13 of my staff up with 40 lbs of bread each to put into the lifeboats. Then I went to help some stewards bring women and children from the lower decks and pushed them in a boat. Afterward, Olaus, I went scouting around, so to speak. Went down to my room and had another hefty drop of liquor. When I went up again on deck I saw that all the boats had gone. So I threw about 50 deck chairs overboard so there'd be something to cling to.

(LIGHTS isolate EVA HART, O. ABELSETH, C. JOUGHIN exit. MUSIC underscores below.)

EVA HART. The band continued to play while all this chaos was about them. It is partly due to their heroism that the passengers didn't panic early on. Now, there is no question that the band played one version of the hymn "Nearer my God to Thee," of which there are three. And the one they played is the one that was played in church. Some months afterwards I was there with my grandmother, and I was so frightened I ran out of church, I knew the tune so well.

*(LIGHTS isolate **LIGHTOLLER**. **EVA HART** exits.)*

LIGHTOLLER. The selfless work of the engine room men can not be praised enough. They struggled to keep the pumps working, and the steam up until the very end; so there would be power for the lights and the wireless.

*(LIGHTS isolate **H. BRIDE**. **LIGHTOLLER** exits.)*

H. BRIDE. The captain came in, and told us "Mr. Bride, Mr. Phillips, you had better get assistance." Mr. Phillips, was the senior Marconi operator, so he went right to work and called "C. Q. D.", the universal distress call.

*(SFX wireless tapping. SLIDE–**MR. PHILLIPS**.)*

He got the Carpathia right away and sent them our position. That fellow, Harold Cottom, the wireless man on the Carpathia, was a great help. Unfortunately, they were over four hours away. But Mr. Phillips kept ticking away messages, always trying to find a closer ship; with me assisting him as I could. Soon the water was pretty close up to the boat deck. There was a great scramble aft and how poor Phillips worked through it, I don't know. I learned to love him that night. I suddenly felt for him a great reverence, to see him there sticking to his work while everyone else was raging about. I will never live to forget the work that Phillips did in those last 15 minutes.

*(LIGHTS shift. SLIDE–**CAPTAIN SMITH. H. BRIDE** turns towards the Slide Image.)*

CAPTAIN SMITH. *(VOICE OVER.)* Men you have done your full duty. You can do no more. Abandon your cabin.

H. BRIDE. But sir, we can stay–

CAPTAIN SMITH. *(VOICE OVER.)* You look out for yourselves. I release you. That's the way of it at this kind of time. Every man for himself.

*(LIGHTS shift. SFX–wireless tapping. SLIDE of **MR PHILLIPS. H. BRIDE** turns towards the Slide Image.)*

H. BRIDE. Then Captain Smith left, but Mr. Phillips went right back to his key.

*(LIGHTS isolate **HAROLD COTTOM. H. BRIDE** exits.)*

H. COTTOM. It was truly providential that the Carpathia received Titanic's message at all. I had the headsets on when I was getting ready to retire for the night. I had just previously called the Parisian and I was waiting for a reply. Had I received it, I should have replied again and would have finished for the night.

*(**H. COTTOM** takes out a paper and looks at it. LIGHTS shift into several Pools of Light revealing **CAPT. ROSTRON** in one area and the **CARPATHIA FIRST OFFICER** in another area. During the below **H. COTTOM** rushes to the **CARPATHIA FIRST OFFICER** then over to **CAPT. ROSTRON** as he is describing it.)*

CAPT. ROSTRON. Harold Cottom, the wireless operator, had taken the message and run with it up to the bridge, gave it to the First Officer, and both ran down the ladder to my door. I had only just turned in. They burst in, which quite irritated me, but before I could reprimand them—

H. COTTOM. Captain Rostron, an urgent message from the Titanic: she's struck a berg and requires immediate assistance! Here's her position.

CAPT. ROSTRON. Turn the ship around.

(CARPATHIA FIRST OFFICER exits.)

Are you absolutely sure it was a distress signal from the Titanic.

H. COTTOM. Yes sir.

CAPT. ROSTRON. You are positive?

H. COTTOM. Absolutely, sir.

CAPT. ROSTRON. Very well, carry on.

(H. COTTOM exits. LIGHTS shift. During the below, CAPT. ROSTRON puts on his Coat & Hat and moves to another part of the stage. Various people come in to take his orders.)

CAPT. ROSTRON. In the meantime I was dressing, and later picked up our position on my chart, and set a course to pick up the Titanic. I then sent for the chief engineer.

(CHIEF ENGINEER & CARPATHIA FIRST OFFICER enter. LIGHTS shift.)

Call another watch of stokers and make all possible speed to the Titanic—she is in trouble.

(CHIEF ENGINEER exits.)

First officer! Knock off all work and prepare all our lifeboats, take out the spare gear, and have them all ready for turning outboard. Have all heads of departments report to me at once.

(CARPATHIA FIRST OFFICER exits. LIGHTS shift to **FIRST CLASS, ISMAY, OFFICER** *and* **THIRD CLASS. CAPT. ROSTRON** *exits.)*

FIRST CLASS. The very model of a decisive leader.

OFFICER. Truly. Due to Captain Rostron's thorough commands–which numbered in the dozens–his ship was fully prepared to receive the survivors.

FIRST CLASS. On top of that, the Carpathia arrived thirty minutes earlier than expected.

ISMAY. And amazingly he was able to keep his own passengers calm.

THIRD CLASS. But the Titanic was close to sinking when Carpathia was still two hours away.

(LIGHTS shift to a dim general wash. **ENSEMBLE** *members are running all over the stage. Soon LIGHTS slowly shift to isolating* **five different areas:**

1. **OFFICER.**

2. **THIRD CLASS** *who is crying and holding a baby. She is talking to a* **STEWARD**–*who is holding her other child.*

3. **JOHN COLLINS.**

4. **RHODA ABBOTT.**

5. **COLONEL GRACIE.**

ENSEMBLE *begins to move in* **slow motion.**)

COLONEL GRACIE. Up from the decks below came a mass of humanity, men and women—and Clinch and I had thought that all the women were already loaded into the boats.

OFFICER. Things became desperate towards the end. Only two collapsible boats were left, and with extreme difficulty, we managed to get them off of the officer's quarters.

R. ABBOTT. I saw the crewman frantically attempting to launch the last two collapsible boats. They managed to get one of them down correctly and we were waiting to board.

J. COLLINS I ran to the port side and found a steward, a woman and her two children. The steward had one of the children in his arms, and the woman was crying.

(J. COLLINS runs over and speaks to THIRD CLASS.)

John Collins, ma'am. Assistant Cook. There's a collapsible boat getting launched.

(He gently takes the baby out of her arms.)

Let's make a go of it.

(J. COLLINS, THIRD CLASS, and STEWARD run to one side of the stage.)

J. COLLINS. The sailors and the firemen that were forward seen the ship's bow in the water and they shouted out for all they were worth that we were to go aft.

(J. COLLINS, STEWARD run off stage. ENSEMBLE freezes in tableau. LIGHTS isolate THIRD CLASS, R. ABBOTT, OFFICER and COLONEL GRACIE.)

THIRD CLASS. We were just turning around to leave when the wave washed us clear off the deck. The last thing I saw was my children washed out of their arms.

*(LIGHTS out on **THIRD CLASS**.)*

OFFICER. The wave pushed off the ship the last two collapsibles—with one of them upside down. I was washed over as well, and pulled under . . .

*(LIGHTS out on **OFFICER**.)*

R. ABBOTT. We were swept away from the deck and . . . I had just enough time to grab hold of my son's hands. Down we were pulled and I struggled with all my might to hold on. But I lost them. I lost them. The sea swallowed them up.

*(LIGHTS out on **R. ABBOTT**.)*

COLONEL GRACIE. The wave came and struck us, and I rose high on the surf, and gave a jump with the water, which took me right on the hurricane deck, where I grabbed an iron railing and held tight. I looked around, and the same wave which saved me engulfed Clinch as well as this vast mass of humanity.

*(LIGHTS dim. **ENSEMBLE** slowly exits.)*

I was thus parted forever from my friend Clinch Smith, with whom I had agreed to remain until the last struggle.

*(Slow BLACKOUT. **COLONEL GRACIE** and **R. ABBOTT** exit. SFX of horrible ship creaks and groans. LIGHTS slowly come back up, dimly on **ISMAY** and **FIRST CLASS**.)*

ISMAY. I can not bear this.

FIRST CLASS. But you shall, Mr. Ismay. You shall.

*(LIGHTS shift and isolate **O. ABELSETH, CHARLES JOUGHIN** and **F. PRENTICE** near the Large Ramp Area. SFX should underscore with panicked people sounds, horrible ship creaks, and everything else that is described below.)*

O. ABELSETH. The bow of the ship was going down, and I asked my cousin and brother-in-law if they could swim and they said no. There was a kind of an explosion—

*(SFX–explosion. **ALL** react. LIGHTS get very dim.)*

C. JOUGHIN.–As if something was buckling; it seemed like the cracking of iron. The ship then gave a great lurch, and a great crowd of people were thrown in a heap—many hundreds of people.

(During above, all three lurch and fall to the ground on to the area that has the ramp at an extreme angle. LIGHTS narrowly isolate this area very dimly. SFX accent the below descriptions.)

O. ABELSETH. The deck raised up and got so steep that people could not stand on their feet on the deck. Many slid on the deck into the water right on the ship. We hung onto a rope in one of the davits.

F. PRENTICE. *(Climbs up the ramp.)* We eventually climbed to the extreme end. I heard crowds of passengers singing hymns just before the vessel went down.

(Hangs behind the back edge of the ramp.)

O. ABELSETH. My brother-in-law said to me, "We had better jump off or the suction will take us down." I said, "No. We won't jump yet. We ain't got much show anyhow, so we might as well stay as long as we can."

*(**J. THAYER** crawls in and slowly crawls up the ramp.)*

C. JOUGHIN. *(Climbs up the ramp.)* I eventually got to the starboard side of the ship and clung to the rail on the outside of the ship.

(Hangs behind the back edge of the ramp.)

J. THAYER. About this time people began jumping from the stern. My friend, Milton Long, and myself stood by each other and jumped on the rail.

(Hangs behind the back edge of the ramp.)

F. PRENTICE. I hung on the rail and then let myself drop into the sea. The distance to the water was quite 75 feet, and I thought I was never going to get there. When I did come into contact with the water it was like a great knife cutting into me. My limbs and body ached for days afterwards.

(He slides backward and disappears, exits.)

J. THAYER. Milton and I did not give each other any messages for back home because neither thought we would ever get back. Hanging over the side, he looked up at me and said, "you are coming, boy, aren't you?" I replied, "go ahead, I'll be with you in a minute." He let go and slid down the side, and I never saw him again.

C. JOUGHIN. I was wondering what next to do when she went down. It felt like riding an elevator. I didn't even go under—my head might have been wet.

*(**C. JOUGHIN & J. THAYER** slide backward and disappear, exit. BLACKOUT. Entire **ENSEMBLE** enters all wearing Lifebelts. SFX–ship sinking sounds. LIGHTS come back up to a dim eerie glow of the stage. **ENSEMBLE** moves in **slow motion** signifying panic in the water. SFX–splashing water and panic sounds. **O. ABELSETH** speaks as he walks slowly through them.)*

O. ABELSETH. It was only about 5 feet down to the water when we jumped off. We then were pulled under, and I swallowed some water.

(BLACKOUT. SFX-swimming under water sounds.)

I got a rope tangled around me, and I let loose of my brother-in-law's hand to get away from the rope. I thought then, "I am a goner." But I came on top again,

(LIGHTS back up to a dim eerie glow.)

and was trying to swim, and there was a man—lots of them were floating around—

*(An **ENSEMBLE MAN** puts his arms around **O. ABELSETH.**)*

And he got me on the neck and pressed me under, trying to get on top of me. But, I got away from him.

(He continues walking.)

I swam, it must have been about 15 or 20 minutes. Then I saw something dark ahead of me. I swam toward that, and it was one of those collapsible boats.

(Crawls into a Lifeboat.)

When I got on this boat, they did not try to push me off. All they said when I got on there was, "Don't capsize the boat."

*(**R. ABBOTT** who was part of the **ENSEMBLE** turns around and slowly walks through the **ENSEMBLE**.)*

R. ABBOTT. I tried in vain to find my dear boys amongst the panicking mass in the water. It was hopeless . . . I had resigned myself to joining them when a strong hand reached out and grabbed my arm.

(O. ABELSETH grabs R. ABBOTT'S arm and pulls her into the Lifeboat.)

This collapsible boat was nearly swamped, but it allowed me to continue on . . . without my boys.

(ENSEMBLE slowly turns their back and remains motionless. At the same time, LIGHTS slowly isolate FIRST CLASS, THIRD CLASS, OFFICER and ISMAY.)

FIRST CLASS. There were some in the lifeboats who could not bear to watch the final plunge. Like yourself, Mr. Ismay. But most were unable to turn away.

THIRD CLASS. They say the last picture was this immense mass of black against the starlit sky . . .

OFFICER. And then nothingness.

ISMAY. Oh God. Oh God . . .

(MUSIC. LIGHTS slowly fade to BLACKOUT.)

CURTAIN

END OF ACT TWO

ACT THREE

AT RISE:

(Act Three begins in total darkness. SFX: Sounds of people yelling and screaming and thrashing about in the ocean. LIGHTS slowly come up to a very dim general wash of the stage. All the ENSEMBLE have on Lifebelts and are spread out around the stage. They are facing ISMAY, who has his back turned to the audience. ENSEMBLE members address their lines towards ISMAY.)

MRS. WHITE. It was something dreadful. We could hear the yells of the steerage passengers as they went down.

D. BUCKLEY. It made a terrible noise, like thunder.

ISMAY. It was absolutely indescribable . . .

FIRST CLASS. *(to ISMAY.)* A sound that has haunted every single survivor.

(ISMAY walks away and sits, visibly shaken. RUTH BECKER and FRANKIE GOLDSMITH approach ISMAY.)

RUTH BECKER. They screamed and they yelled for help. And of course nobody came to help. That was a terrible, terrible time. I can still hear them.

F. GOLDSMITH. I used to live near Navin Field, a baseball field in Detroit, and every time a homerun was hit and I would hear the crowd break into a roar I'd think of the Titanic; because that's what it sounded like. Those people–hundreds and hundreds of people–in the water.

(LIGHTS shift.)

FIRST CLASS. Those in the Lifeboats had a terrible decision to make.

THIRD CLASS. And in almost all cases, the decision was 'no'.

(LAWRENCE BEESLEY approaches ISMAY.)

L. BEESLEY. We wished with all our hearts to return and rescue some people, but we knew it could not be done. Our boat was filled to capacity and if we had returned it would have meant the swamping of everyone on board. We attempted to sing to keep us from thinking about them, but there was no heart for singing. . .

(MR. HERBERT PITMAN approaches ISMAY. L. BEESLEY exits.)

MR. H. PITMAN. As soon as she disappeared I said, "Now, men, we will pull toward the wreck. We may be able to pick up a few more." Everyone in my boat said it was a mad idea, because we had far better save what few we had in my boat than go back and be swamped by the crowds.

(LIGHTS shift. MR. H. PITMAN exits.)

FIRST CLASS. The women tried to convince themselves that it was not their husbands they were hearing.

(MRS. WHITE and THOMAS JONES approaches ISMAY.)

MRS. WHITE. Thomas Jones, the man in charge of our boat, urged us to go back, but only one of the ladies agreed. I remember his disappointed look.

T. JONES. I said to them "Ladies, if any of us are saved, remember I wanted to go back. I would rather drown with them than leave them."

(He exits.)

MRS. WHITE. We kept pulling for the mysterious light for thirty minutes, never getting any closer. We then decided to stop and go back. But, we could not find anyone.

(JACK THAYER approaches ISMAY.)

J. THAYER. The partially filled lifeboats standing by only a few hundred yards away never came back. Why on earth they did not come back is a mystery. How could any human being fail to heed those cries?

ISMAY. We couldn't . . .

(MRS. RYERSON approaches ISMAY.)

MRS. RYERSON. We turned to pick up some of those in the water. Some of the women protested, but others persisted, and we dragged in six or seven men who were so chilled and frozen already they could hardly move. Two of them died in the stern later and many were raving and moaning and delirious most of the time.

OFFICER. Only one lifeboat ventured forth into the mass of humanity in the water.

THIRD CLASS. But they were too late.

(LIGHTS isolate MR. LOWE. During his monologue, the ENSEMBLE spreads out all around the stage. FIRST CLASS and THIRD CLASS escort ISMAY to a place amongst the ENSEMBLE.)

MR. LOWE. As soon as I could, I herded ours and four other lifeboats, together and roped them up. Of course I had to wait until the yells and shrieks had subsided—for the people to thin out—and then I deemed it safe for me to go amongst the wreckage. I transferred all 53 passengers from my boat. It was at this time that I found this Italian. He had a shawl over his head. I pulled this shawl off his face and saw he was a man. He was in a great hurry to get into the other boat, and I caught hold of him and pitched him in; because he was not worthy of being handled better. I then asked for volunteers to go with me to the wreck. Mr. Crowe?

(MR. G. CROWE joins MR. LOWE in his lighted area. ENSEMBLE slowly turns their backs to the Audience.)

MR. G. CROWE. Officer Lowe impressed upon us that we must go back to the wreck. But there was no protest whatever. In fact a second-class passenger named Norris Williams,

(NORRIS WILLIAMS enters and joins him.)

the champion racket player of England, returned with us. There were also two seaman, Frank Evans

(FRANK EVANS crosses and joins them.)

and Edward Buley.

(EDWARD BULEY crosses and joins them.)

(BLACKOUT. Slight Pause. MR. G. CROWE, MR. LOWE, F. EVANS, E. BULEY, and N. WILLIAMS sit/stand in a small area. Their FLASHLIGHTS are the only LIGHTS that are seen. ALL other ENSEMBLE members–including ISMAY–stand with their backs to the Audience in tableau, moving very slightly, as if bobbing dead in the water.)

F. EVANS. We went straight over toward the wreckage and soon had picked up three men alive, though one died on the way back.

E. BULEY. When we picked him up he was bleeding from the mouth and nose.

MR. LOWE. I propped him up at the stern of the boat, and tried to give him every chance to breathe; but, unfortunately, he died.

E. BULEY. As we continued searching–

VOICE 1. Help . . . Please . . .

E. BULEY.–We suddenly heard another voice calling for help. We looked around and could make out a figure kneeling on a piece of wreckage.

F. EVANS. The man told me later that he jumped as the ship had started to plunge. He eventually crawled aboard a piece of paneling along with another man. He said his companion grew weaker through the night until he muttered "what a night" and rolled off dead.

N. WILLIAMS. There were plenty of dead bodies about us. You couldn't hardly count them. I was afraid to look over the sides because it might break my nerves down.

VOICE 2. Over here. . .

MR. LOWE. We searched and searched–

VOICE 3. Please help . . .

MR. LOWE.–hearing cries here and there–

VOICE 4. Don't leave . . .

MR. LOWE.–but never finding them.

VOICE 5. Oh God . . .

E. BULEY. There were a good few dead. Of course you could not discern them exactly on account of the wreckage; but we turned over several of them to see if they were alive. They all had life preservers on.

F. EVANS. They simply had perished.

N. WILLIAMS. It looked as though none of them were drowned. It looked as though they were frozen altogether.

F. EVANS. Most of the dead I saw in the water were men.

MR. LOWE. I did not see a single female body, not one, around the wreckage.

MR. LOWE, F. EVANS, E. BULEY, N. WILLIAMS *(Staggered.)* I will never forget it 'till my dying day.

(FLASHLIGHTS Out. Pause. MUSIC bridge. **ENSEMBLE** *exits. LIGHTS slowly up on the Hearing with* **MR. LOWE & S. SMITH.***)*

MR. LOWE. We picked up a total of four from the water, and the one died. I then left the wreck.

S. SMITH. You said you laid off a bit to wait until it quieted down. Until what quieted down?

MR. LOWE. Until the drowning people had thinned out.

S. SMITH. But your boat had a water capacity of 65 people?

MR. LOWE. Yes, but then what are you going to do with a boat of 65 where 1,500 people are drowning?

S. SMITH. You could have saved 15.

MR. LOWE. You could not do it, sir.

S. SMITH. At least, you made no attempt to do it?

MR. LOWE. I made the attempt, sir, as soon as any man could do so, and I am not scared of saying it. I did not hang back or anything else.

S. SMITH. I am not saying you hung back. I am just saying–

MR. LOWE. You had to do so. It was absolutely useless for me to go into the mass. It would have been suicide.

S. SMITH. About how long did you lay by?

MR. LOWE. I should say an hour and a half.

S. SMITH. You were about approximately 150 yards from the ship?

MR. LOWE. I was just on the margin. If anybody had struggled out of the mass, I was there to pick them up, because we could have handled them there. We could never have handled them in the mass.

*(LIGHTS shift. **S. SMITH & MR. LOWE** exit.)*

ISMAY. It was such a long night . . .

FIRST CLASS. Twenty lifeboats floating helplessly in the water.

OFFICER. Most of which were isolated from the others.

THIRD CLASS. And very few people knew about the approaching rescue ship.

*(During the below scenes and monologues, **ENSEMBLE** members should enter just prior to their scene. Each section should be played in a different part of the stage. LIGHTS shift and isolate **MRS. DOUGLAS** and **CREWMAN**.)*

MRS. DOUGLAS. I was in a boat with dozens of men—they had been picked up from the London unemployed to fill out the crew. These men would not row, told frightful stories to alarm us, and when the Carpathia was sighted—

CREWMAN. We are jolly lucky. No work tonight; nothing to do but smoke and yarn. Back in London next week with the unemployed.

MRS. DOUGLAS. All the women told of insufficient seamen to man the boats; all women rowed; some had to bail water from their boats. Mrs. Smith was told to watch a cork in her boat, and if it came out to put her finger in place of it.

*(LIGHTS isolate **RUTH BECKER & LEAH AKS. MRS. DOUGLAS** and **CREWMAN** exit.)*

RUTH BECKER. There was a German woman with us who had been sobbing.

LEAH AKS. My tiny baby was torn away from me and tossed into another lifeboat! I tried to retrieve him but I was kept back by a crewman. He thought I was rushing the boat!

(Sobs.)

RUTH BECKER. *(To **LEAH AKS**.)* I promise I will help you find your baby when we are rescued.

(Pause.)

Little did I know then, that the baby had been thrown into No.11, the boat my mother was on.

*(To **LEAH AKS**.)*

Ruth Becker.

LEAH AKS. Leah Aks.

*(LIGHTS shift to the **DUFF GORDONS**, a **FEMALE ENSEMBLE MEMBER** and **ROBERT PUSEY. RUTH BECKER** and **LEAH AKS** exit.)*

LADY DUFF GORDON. Oh Laura, there is your beautiful nightdress gone.

R. PUSEY. Never mind that, Mrs. Duff Gordon, you've got your life.

(She reacts. Pause.)

I suppose you've lost everything?

SIR DUFF GORDON. Of course.

R. PUSEY. Well we have lost all our kit and the company won't give us any more. What's more, our pay stops from tonight. All they'll do is send us back to London . . .

SIR DUFF GORDON. You fellows need not worry about that, I will give you a fiver each to start a new kit.

R. PUSEY. Thank you sir!

*(LIGHTS isolate **MRS. WHITE. DUFF GORDONS** and **R. PUSEY** exit.)*

MRS. WHITE. The lamp on our boat was absolutely worth nothing. I had a cane with an electric light in it and that was the only light we had. The men in our boat were anything but seamen, with the exception of one man. The women all rowed—every one of them. The men did not know the first thing about it. Even Miss Young rowed, except when she was throwing up, which she did six or seven times. Where would we have been if it had not been for our women? Our head seaman would give an order and those men who knew nothing would say, "If you don't stop talking there will be one less in the boat." We were in the hands of men of that kind. I never saw a finer body of men in my life than the men passengers on this trip—athletes and men of sense—and if they had been permitted to enter these lifeboats with their families the boats would have been appropriately manned and many more lives saved.

(LIGHTS isolate **MRS. HELEN BISHOP. MRS. WHITE** *exits.)*

MRS. BISHOP. Here we were in the middle of the freezing Atlantic with no compass, no light, and I do not know about the crackers or water. We were totally separated from all of the boats except the one tied to us. But I must say, the crewmen in our boat were wonderful. One man lost his brother. When the Titanic was going down I remember he just put his hand over his face; and immediately after she sank he did the best he could to keep the women feeling cheerful all the rest of the time. We all thought a great deal of that man.

(LIGHTS isolate **MR. H. PITMAN & T. JONES** *talking together.* **MRS. BISHOP** *exits.)*

MR. H. PITMAN. Thomas, in our lifeboat there was a man holding a revolver, which I guess he had on him. He was talking to a man who had been rubbing his fiancée's wet stocking feet—

(LIGHTS come up dimly on **TWO ENSEMBLE MEN** *talking to one another.)*

MAN. Should the worse come to the worst, you can use this revolver for your wife. After my wife and I have finished with it.

(LIGHTS out on the **MEN.** *They exit.)*

MR. H. PITMAN. And he said it so calmly like! I didn't say anything as I was the only one to overhear him, I think.

T. JONES. There was a strong woman at the oar with me in lifeboat number 8, and she was helping me every minute. It was she who suggested we should sing.

MR. H. PITMAN. Sing, you say!?

T. JONES. I should think we did, Herbert! It kept up our spirits. We sang as we rowed, all of us, starting with "Pull for the Shore", and we were still singing when we saw the lights of the Carpathia. Then we stopped singing, and prayed.

(LIGHTS shift to an area near one of the Lifeboats. MOLLY BROWN, MAJOR PEUCHEN and MR. ROBERT HITCHENS are there. MR. H. PITMAN and T. JONES exit.)

MOLLY BROWN. Let me tell you a thing or two about that Hitchens fellow. I knew we were in trouble from the moment Major Peuchen got into our boat.

MAJOR PEUCHEN. What do you want me—

MR. HITCHENS. Hurry up. This boat is going to founder.

(MR. HITCHENS pushes him into the Lifeboat then crosses over to another part of the stage. The Hearing LIGHTS slowly come up. S. SMITH. enters.)

MAJOR PEUCHEN. I thought he meant our lifeboat, but he meant the Titanic was going to founder. So we got the rudder in, and he told me to go forward and take an oar.

(During the below, S. SMITH and MR. HITCHENS freeze when MOLLY BROWN & MAJOR PEUCHEN are speaking. MR. HITCHENS turns towards MOLLY BROWN and MAJOR PEUCHEN when he speaks to them.)

S. SMITH. Did you have any trouble with the major, between the Titanic and the Carpathia?

MR. HITCHENS. Only once, sir. He was not in the boat more than 10 minutes before he wanted to come and take charge.

S. SMITH. What did you say to him?

*(LIGHTS shift, **MR. HITCHENS** turns and speaks to **MOLLY BROWN** and **MAJOR PEUCHEN**.)*

MR. HITCHENS. I am put here in charge of the boat. You go and do what you are told to do!

*(LIGHTS shift, **MR. HITCHENS** turns back to Hearing.)*

S. SMITH. Did he say anything more to you?

MR. HITCHENS. He did not answer me, sir, but sat down, alongside of Seaman Fleet, who was doing most of the work himself.

S. SMITH. Go on.

MR. HITCHENS. Everybody seemed in a very bad condition in the boat, sir, but we were in a dangerous place, so I told them to man the oars, ladies and all. "All of you do your best." I said. We started going after this light.

*(LIGHTS shift, **MR. HITCHENS & S. SMITH** freeze.)*

MOLLY BROWN. He wasn't giving us any pep talk. It was more like a little sergeant barking commands. He wasn't letting the ladies row, either.

MAJOR PEUCHEN. Indeed not, Mrs. Brown. I recall that as we pulled away there was a sort of a whistle. The quartermaster told us to stop rowing so he could hear it, and then there was a call for help, from a megaphone, I believe. This was the Captain calling us to come back to the ship. We all thought we ought to go, but—

*(LIGHTS shift, **MR. HITCHENS** turns towards them.)*

MR. HITCHENS. No, we are not going back. It is our lives now, not theirs. We need to row farther away!

*(LIGHTS shift, **MR. HITCHENS** turns back to Hearing.)*

MR. HITCHENS. I was following the Captain's last orders: pull for the light, which we thought to be a sailing ship. Besides, I couldn't see who was yelling at us.

*(LIGHTS shift, **MR. HITCHENS & S. SMITH** pantomime talking.)*

MAJOR PEUCHEN. I did not say anything. I knew I was perfectly powerless. He was at the rudder.

MOLLY BROWN. Well, our boat was just creeping along with just those two men rowing—and we were all freezing like nothing else—so I grabbed an oar, put it in an oarlock, and told Miss Martin to hold it while I put one in on the other side. Then before I knew it, that girl was pulling like the best of them! Then I sat down and started in.

MAJOR PEUCHEN. The Quartermaster could do nothing to stop the other women from joining in. So—

*(LIGHTS shift, **MR. HITCHENS** turns towards them.)*

MR. HITCHENS. Hurry up you lot! The suction is going to pull everything down for miles around! Pull, pull, pull! Unless you want to be around when the boilers explode.

MOLLY BROWN. He would always harp on that gruesome stuff when ever he thought the women were getting tired.

MAJOR PEUCHEN. I asked him to come and assist us in rowing, and let some woman steer the boat, as it was a perfectly calm night. He refused to do it.

(LIGHTS shift to Hearing.)

MR. HITCHENS. I would rather be pulling the boat than be steering. But I seen no one there to steer, so I thought, being in charge of the boat, it was the best way to steer myself.

MAJOR PEUCHEN. He also asked one of the ladies for some brandy, and for one of her wraps, which he got.

MR. HITCHENS. Mrs. Mayer was rather vexed with me and I spoke rather straight to her—she accused me of wrapping myself up blankets, using bad language, and drinking all the whisky, which I deny, sir.

MOLLY BROWN. Not only did he demand the blanket, but he guzzled the whisky like there was no tomorrow!

MR. HITCHENS. We stopped pulling when I reckoned we'd never reach the other ship. At that time we were a mile or more away from the Titanic. Probably 10 minutes after that, her lights disappeared, but I did not see her go down.

MOLLY BROWN. Then that horrible screaming started.

MR. HITCHENS. I did not hear any cries as regarding distress. We did hear a lot of crying and screaming.

MOLLY BROWN. Some of us begged the quartermaster to return.

(LIGHTS shift.)

MR. HITCHENS. It is no use going back, there's only a lot of stiffs there! Those that are left will swamp us for sure!

MOLLY BROWN. I should have socked him one for that.

MAJOR PEUCHEN. I said to the women, "It is no use arguing with that man. It is best not to discuss matters with him." So, we did not return to the boat.

MOLLY BROWN. No. We didn't go back.

(LIGHTS shift.)

S. SMITH. During the time that you were lying off of your oars, did the women in your boat urge you to go toward the wreckage?

MR. HITCHENS. Not that I remember, sir. I am not aware of it.

S. SMITH. And you wish the committee to understand that you did not refuse to go to the relief of people in the water?

MR. HITCHENS. I could not, sir. I was too far away, and I had no compass to go back, to enable me to find where the cries came from. The cries I heard lasted about two minutes–

MOLLY BROWN. It lasted an hour!

MR. HITCHENS.–And some of the men in the boat said it was the cries of one boat hailing the other. I suppose the reason they said this was not to alarm the ladies in the boat.

S. SMITH. I see. What happened later?

MR. HITCHENS. Well, when the light on the horizon eventually disappeared, I did my best to keep up spirits.

*(LIGHTS shift. **MR. HITCHENS** turns. **S. SMITH** exits.)*

MR. HITCHENS. We're going to drift for days. Out here, hundreds of miles from land with no water, food, or protection of any kind!

MOLLY BROWN. He had a knack for making a terrible situation worse.

MAJOR PEUCHEN. I have done a good deal of yachting in my life, and I can tell you the man did not know anything about navigating. At one point he saw another light, a reflection really, and he thought it might be a buoy!

MOLLY BROWN. Amazing . . .

MAJOR PEUCHEN. We soon found another lifeboat and hitched our boat to it. By this time, Mrs. Brown had parceled out parts of her clothing to others who were freezing. You even gave your sable to an under-dressed stoker!

MOLLY BROWN. All I was doing was trying to jolly everyone along until we were rescued. After a while, we started to see the rockets being fired by the Carpathia.

MR. HITCHENS. They are just shooting stars!

MOLLY BROWN. At daybreak we saw the Carpathia heave into sight.

MAJOR PEUCHEN. Someone asked him if the ship was going to rescue us.

MR. HITCHENS. No, she is not going to pick us up. She is to pick up the bodies!

MAJOR PEUCHEN. He had no intention of going towards the Carpathia.

(MOLLY BROWN & MAJOR PEUCHEN cross towards MR. HITCHENS.)

MOLLY BROWN. Well, that was it for me. I wasn't going to sit there and hope we'd be found. So I got Helen Candee and the other ladies rallied together, and we cut loose from the other boat and started rowing hard and fast.

MR. HITCHENS. I will not have this! I am in command of this vessel!

(MR. HITCHENS continues grumbling, underscoring the below.)

MAJOR PEUCHEN. The ladies kept telling him they were freezing, and wanted to make sure our lifeboat would not be missed. But he kept ranting–

MR. HITCHENS. If you don't shut that hole in your face–

(MOLLY BROWN gets close to him.)

MOLLY BROWN. Now you listen to me, sonny. You make one more move to stop us and I'm throwing you overboard!

(MR. HITCHENS pulls away, sits down.)

MAJOR PEUCHEN. He was clearly broken by this and sank under his blanket, frightened.

MOLLY BROWN. He was shaking like an aspen! But he kept on swearing and insulting me. I didn't really care; we were finally moving again.

MAJOR PEUCHEN. From that point on, "The Unsinkable" Molly Brown was in charge of the boat!

(LIGHTS isolate MR. HITCHENS.)

MR. HITCHENS. All those statements against me are false. I think it was very unkind of them to make any statements criticizing me.

*(LIGHTS shift, **MOLLY BROWN** moves closer and gives **MR. HITCHENS** the eye. **MR. HITCHENS** runs off stage. BLACKOUT. **MOLLY BROWN & MAJOIR PEUCHEN** exit. MUSIC Bridge. LIGHTS Eventually come up dimly on one of the Lifeboats with **O. ABELSETH, AUGUST WENNERSTROM, RHODA ABBOTT** and some **ENSEMBLE** members.)*

O. ABELSETH. In this little boat they called Collapsible A, we tried to raise the canvas up, but we could not get it up. We stood all night, more than four hours, in about 14 inches of water. I was continually moving my arms and swinging them around to keep warm.

A. WENNERSTROM. My friends Gerda and Edvard Lindell swam with me to the boat. Poor Gerda did not have the strength to climb aboard. But eventually Edvard and I were able too. I continued to hold onto Gerda to keep her afloat. But soon she passed away. I turned and saw Edvard. His face was sunken and his eyes had changed . . . I knew then he was dead and I gently pushed him over the side to join his wife.

R. ABBOTT. Three of the men sustained their life by punching each other during the hours they stood up.

A. WENNERSTROM. All the feeling left us. If we wanted to know if we still had legs left, we had to feel down into the water with our hand.

O. ABELSETH. Thirty or so started on this raft but only twelve lasted.

A. WENNERSTROM. The only exercise we got was when someone gave up hope and died, we then immediately threw them overboard to give the live ones a little more space and at the same time lighten the weight of the boat.

R. ABBOTT. The minute any one got tired and sat down in the water, shortly thereafter, they floated off the raft, dead.

O. ABELSETH. One man sitting behind me complained of cramps and put his arms around me for warmth. After he died, I had to pry his arms loose. There was another man I tried to keep alive; but I could not make it. It was just at the break of day, and I took him by the shoulder and raised him up, so that he was sitting up. I said to him, "We can see a ship now. Brace up."

MAN. Who are you? Let me be. Who are you?

O. ABELSETH. It was not about half an hour or so when he died.

R. ABBOTT. I have little memory of being transferred into Officer Lowe's boat several hours later. But I was told that a Fireman named Trefall cradled me in his arms until I was lifted aboard the Carpathia . . .

*(LIGHTS shift, very dimly isolating **H. BRIDE** on the highest platform. **O. ABELSETH, A. WENNER-STROM, R. ABBOTT, MAN** exit.)*

H. BRIDE. I happened to be nearest overturned Collapsible B, grabbed it and went over with it when the wave hit. I found myself underneath, inside the boat. I remained there, I don't know how long. It seemed a lifetime to me, really.

*(LIGHTS shift, very dimly come up on **LIGHTOLLER**. SFX during all of the below. During the BLACKOUTS there should be SFX sounds of a person being underwater.)*

LIGHTOLLER. The Titanic took a dive, and I turned face forward and also took a dive. Striking the water was like a thousand knives being driven into my body. I was then sucked underwater and pulled against this grating on an air shaft.

(BLACKOUT. SFX sounds of a person being underwater.)

I struggled and kicked for all I was worth, but it was impossible to get away—with every instant expecting the wire to go and find myself shot down into the bowels of the ship.

*(LIGHTS very dimly come up on **COLONEL GRACIE**.)*

COLONEL GRACIE. I was taken down with the ship, but I soon let go of the railing.

(BLACKOUT. SFX sounds of a person being underwater.)

I felt myself whirled around, swam under water, fearful that the hot water that came up from the boilers might boil me up, and succeeded finally in reaching the surface.

LIGHTOLLER. This explosion took place and there was a terrific blast of hot air and water which blew me clear.

*(LIGHTS very dimly come up **LIGHTOLLER**.)*

I just managed to gulp some air before I was pulled down again against the fiddly gratings.

(BLACKOUT. SFX sounds of a person being underwater.)

LIGHTOLLER. I am still unsure exactly how I got clear of this grating, but I did.

J. COLLINS. I was down for at least two minutes under the water.

*(LIGHTS shift, very dimly come up **JOHN COLLINS**.)*

When I came to the surface I saw this boat was only about 4 or 5 yards off of it, and I swam over to it.

(He slowly walks towards the highest platform.)

*(LIGHTS very dimly come up on **COLONEL GRACIE**.)*

COLONEL GRACIE. When I came up to the surface there was no ship there and all around me was wreckage. I saw what seemed to be bodies all around. These bodies... drowning people . . . gasping for breath . . .

(He slowly walks towards the highest platform.)

*(LIGHTS shift, very dimly come up on **LIGHTOLLER**.)*

LIGHTOLLER. When I resurfaced, I saw the overturned collapsible and grabbed a piece of rope attached to it and floated along.

(He slowly walks towards the highest platform. SFX during below.)

Just then, the forward funnel fell alongside coming within inches of myself and the lifeboat.

(BLACKOUT. SFX sounds of a person being underwater.)

It fell right amongst the struggling mass of humanity in the water, killing many of them. It also caused a huge wave that washed the boat and myself at least fifty yards clear of the ship.

(LIGHTS very dimly come up on Highest Platform.)

Slowly many people surfaced, and all of us began crawling atop it.

J. COLLINS. Nobody helped me. But I got onto it.

(He does.)

They were all watching the ship.

COLONEL GRACIE. I grabbed the arm of someone and pulled myself up on this boat.

*(He does. Other **MALE ENSEMBLE** members attempt to do so as well, including **C. JOUGHIN**.)*

H. BRIDE. Eventually, I freed myself from under it and cleared out. I then swam back and there was just room for me to crawl on the edge.

(He does.)

COLONEL GRACIE. We loaded the boat until we could take no more.

H. BRIDE. There was a big crowd on top when I got on and I was the last man they invited on board.

*(Some **ENSEMBLE MEMBERS** are pushed away, though a couple still hold on, one of which is **C. JOUGHIN**.)*

CREWMAN. Don't you think we ought to pray?

H. BRIDE. Each man called out his religion.

*(**ENSEMBLE** does.)*

It was decided to do the Lord's Prayer. We spoke it over in chorus.

*(**ENSEMBLE** does, underscoring the below.)*

H. BRIDE. Soon after, I saw dozens of others in the water struggling to get on. It was a terrible sight.

LIGHTOLLER. We had gathered three bits of wood and were using them as makeshift oars.

COLONEL GRACIE. Our concern now was to get out of the wreckage and away from the swimmers in the water before they tried to get on the boat, and all of us would be lost.

LIGHTOLLER. I eventually took command of the men, as was necessary for survival.

COLONEL GRACIE. We were taken away from the screams of the drowning people, and we were on the lookout then for lights and ships to come to our rescue.

LIGHTOLLER. Bride informed me which rescue ships were on their way.

H. BRIDE. I called for Phillips several times, but got no response.

LIGHTOLLER. I had the men all stand up.

*(They **ALL** slowly stand up.)*

*(**ALL** pantomime the descriptions below.)*

COLONEL GRACIE. We had to keep the equilibrium while standing up all the time.

LIGHTOLLER. I had them lean to the left or right, depending on the waves.

COLONEL GRACIE. If one of us had fallen, we would have fallen to our knees, and then to the water, and that would have been the end of us.

LIGHTOLLER. When one man would fall over from exhaustion or exposure, another one would be allowed on board.

*(One **MALE ENSEMBLE** falls over, another comes up.)*

H. BRIDE. There were several men hanging onto the sides, hoping for a chance to board.

J. COLLINS. We were all telling this one man not to get on. If he had caught hold of her he would have tumbled the whole lot of us off.

MAN. *(VOICE OVER.)* That is all right, boys, keep cool. God bless you, and good-bye.

J. COLLINS. He swam along for about two minutes. Then we were washed out of his road. I . . . I was still thinking on the child that was washed out of my arms . . .

LIGHTOLLER. How anyone survived the night is nothing short of miraculous. Some quietly lost consciousness and slipped overboard. No one was in a condition to help.

C. JOUGHIN. I had been treading water for about two hours or so when I was rescued by Collapsible B. There was no room for me but I tried to climb aboard. Someone pushed me from it, and then a chap who knew me gave me a hand and helped to hold me up. The edge of my lifebelt rested on the edge of the boat.

COLONEL GRACIE. As the sun came up, a welcome sight was four lifeboats on our starboard side. Lightoller blew his whistle and ordered them to come over and take us off. They immediately turned toward us.

LIGHTOLLER. Before our rescue we had seen the rockets from the Carpathia, and were praying to God we'd not be missed.

COLONEL GRACIE. The two boats came right up close and then began the difficult task of a transfer. The lifeboat I was put on was filled up to 65.

*(They **ALL** slowly and with difficulty start to exit.)*

C. JOUGHIN. After being in the water all that time, I actually felt colder when I got into the lifeboat.

H. BRIDE. I heard afterwards that Mr. Phillips was on board, but he. . . he expired before we were taken off the overturned boat.

*(BLACKOUT. MUSIC bridge. LIGHTS come up on **ISMAY, FIRST CLASS, THIRD CLASS,** and **OFFICER.**)*

ISMAY. Overwhelming . . . All these dreadful experiences.

FIRST CLASS. Yes, Mr. Ismay. Your time aboard Collapsible C pales in comparison, does it not?

(ISMAY nods his head and has tears in his eyes.)

FIRST CLASS. Ah . . . A side of Bruce Ismay the world has never seen . . .

(ISMAY turns away. Pause. LIGHTS Shift and isolate LAWRENCE BEESLEY.)

L. BEESLEY. When first we saw the Carpathia, it was just a light, creeping over the edge of the sea, and soon a second below it. It seemed almost too good to be true. I believe all of us had tears in our eyes. Shouts and cheers were heard all around us

(LIGHTS Shift and isolate MRS. RYERSON. L. BEESLEY exits.)

MRS. RYERSON. When the sun rose we saw the Carpathia standing up about 5 miles away, and for the first time saw the icebergs all around us.

(LIGHTS shift and isolate MRS. DOUGLAS. MRS. RYERSON exits.)

MRS. DOUGLAS. When we pulled alongside the Carpathia, I blurted out, "The Titanic has gone down with everyone on board", and Mr. Boxhall told me to "shut up." This is not told in criticism; I think he was perfectly right. They threw down rope ladders, and all that could had to climb up in mid ocean on a swaying rope ladder.

(LIGHTS shift and isolate EVA HART & RUTH BECKER talking together.)

EVA HART. I was a mere seven years old at the time, so I couldn't climb up a rope ladder. So they got these big luggage nets, and the mesh is very wide apart so the children would have legs and feet slipping through. So each child was put into a sack. Ruth, I remember being petrified when I was put in that sack, and it was tied round. The sack full of these children was put into these huge nets and hauled aboard.

*(LIGHTS shift and isolate **JOHN THOMPSON** & **KATE BUSS** talking together.)*

J. THOMPSON. Miss Buss, My jaw was locked tight from the cold and when I tried to climb the ladder, I discovered that I must have broken my arm when the ship foundered. There was another bloke whose feet were so swollen they had busted out of his shoes. So, they threw down a rope for both of us, we slung it under our arms, and we were hoisted up.

K. BUSS. Oh, Mr. Thompson, I was so fearful of heights that I held back, continually finding an excuse not to leave the lifeboat. When another woman slipped and dangled by the safety rope, my terror deepened. When I was the last woman in the boat, I forced myself to climb, not daring to ever look down. When finally I stepped onto the deck, I heard a voice cry out "Bring out the swings! No more ladders!" And with that, I began laughing hysterically and buried my face in the blanket they had wrapped around me.

*(LIGHTS shift back to **MRS. DOUGLAS. K. BUSS** & **J. THOMPSON** exit.)*

MRS. DOUGLAS. I asked a chief steward to take the news to Captain Rostron. But he said Officer Boxhall was with him.

*(LIGHTS shift and isolate **CAPT. ROSTRON** talking to **MR. BOXHALL. MRS. DOUGLAS** exits.)*

CAPT. ROSTRON. Your ship is gone?

MR. BOXHALL. Yes, she went down at about 2:20.

CAPT. ROSTRON. Were many people left on board when she sank?

MR. BOXHALL. Hundreds and hundreds! Perhaps a thousand! My God, sir, they've gone down with her! They couldn't live in this icy cold water!

CAPT. ROSTRON. Thank you, mister!

(Pause. Gentler.)

Go below and get some coffee, and try to keep warm.

*(LIGHTS shift back to **RUTH BECKER & EVA HART**. **MR. BOXHALL** and **CAPT. ROSTRON** exit.)*

RUTH BECKER. Eva, do you remember as soon as we were on board the women all standing at the rails watching for their husbands to come in later boats?

EVA HART. I shall never forget it. And of course so many never came. I couldn't find my mother, and I didn't find her for hours.

*(MUSIC plays. **ALL ENSEMBLE MEMBERS** enter and go to different areas of the stage. **FEMALE ENSEMBLE MEMBERS** are searching for their husbands. **MALE ENSEMBLE MEMBERS** are in a daze. **MOLLY BROWN** is going around offering comfort. **ISMAY** walks amongst the **ENSEMBLE** unseen, experiencing this scene. Eventually, **ALL FEMALE ENSEMBLE MEMBERS** realize their husbands are gone and seek comfort in each other. LIGHTS slowly go to BLACKOUT as the MUSIC continues. After a few moments, LIGHTS*

*isolate **THIRD CLASS, ISMAY, OFFICER,** and **FIRST CLASS. ENSEMBLE** freezes.)*

FIRST CLASS. Your isolation prevented you from bearing witness, Mr. Ismay.

THIRD CLASS. But absolution comes with a price.

ISMAY. I grieve beside these heartsick widows.

THIRD CLASS. As did the passengers on board the Carpathia.

FIRST CLASS. They treated the survivors with much kindness and gave them every comfort possible.

OFFICER. While looming in the distance people could see 13 icebergs and miles of floating ice in every direction. The Carpathia had near misses with no less than five icebergs on her way towards us.

*(LIGHTS isolate **MRS. DOUGLAS. ENSEMBLE** slowly exits in despair.)*

MRS. DOUGLAS. When we sailed away, the ship circled the point where the Titanic had gone down, and I searched vainly for a glimmer of hope, but saw nothing except quantities of loose cork floating in the current, like a stream—nothing else.

*(LIGHTS isolate **RUTH DODGE. MRS. DOUGLAS** exits.)*

RUTH DODGE. I was one of the few women to find my husband safe on the Carpathia. I'd been searching for hours when finally my four-year-old son told me he'd seen him! He thought it would be game to hide from him. He never could understand why I was so angry when he finally announced "I have seen Daddy!"

*(LIGHTS isolate **RUTH BECKER. RUTH DODGE** exits.)*

RUTH BECKER. On the voyage home, I was frequently asked "How did it happen your entire family was saved?" To which I simply answered "Providence". Others hid their pain by jokingly accusing me of saving more than my share. One bright spot came when I discovered that my friend Leah Aks had found her missing child.

*(LIGHTS isolate **F. GOLDSMITH. RUTH BECKER** exits.)*

F. GOLDSMITH. My mother had put me under the helpful eye of Samuel Collins. It had been just a few days earlier I'd seen him stoking the boilers on the Titanic. He was a marvelous fellow! He took me down to visit the Carpathia's stokers and they all rallied around and decided to make me an "honorary seaman". Ah, but it wasn't that easy! To achieve this lofty title, they made me drink a nasty concoction of vinegar, water, and a raw egg! They called it a Bombay Oyster. And don't you know—I downed it in one swallow!

*(LIGHTS isolate **THIRD CLASS, ISMAY, OFFICER,** and **FIRST CLASS. F. GOLDSMITH** exits.)*

THIRD CLASS. Even with deep kindness being displayed at every turn, the class discrimination was still in full force.

*(LIGHTS isolate **AMY STANLEY**.)*

AMY STANLEY. When I boarded the Carpathia I was wearing the only fur coat I owned. So, they immediately assumed I was part of the "upper class" and proceeded to give me a berth in a cabin! But it was short lived. They soon discovered their error and gave my space to an older woman who officially was "first class". Imagine!

*(LIGHTS isolate **THIRD CLASS, ISMAY, OFFICER,** and **FIRST CLASS. AMY STANLEY** exits.)*

ISMAY. That should never have happened.

THIRD CLASS. No, it should not.

FIRST CLASS. Margaret "Molly" Brown, however, was an absolute saint aboard the Carpathia. She comforted everyone she came across—often speaking to people in their native languages. She also helped sew blankets into clothing for the poor, and sent telegrams to families.

OFFICER. Meanwhile, the dreadful news slowly made its way to the world.

*(LIGHTS dim. Short MUSIC bridge. LIGHTS slowly isolate **STEPHEN TOWNSEND**. In another dimmer pool of LIGHT, **MRS. A. E. LEWIS** and **DOROTHY CROSS** are talking to each other.)*

S. TOWNSEND. When the news reached Southampton on Tuesday morning, a sickening dread fell over the town.

MRS. A. E. LEWIS. *(Reading newspaper.)* Tuesday was a day of gloom, such as never before experienced in living memory.

S. TOWNSEND. There wasn't a family in that whole area that didn't have somebody associated with that ship. Hundreds of women with children in tow rushed to where White Star Line Offices were. It was real panic. Everybody, everybody was in distress. And they all spent, oh, hours and hours down there.

D. CROSS. *(Reading newspaper.)* A great hush has descended on our town.

S. TOWNSEND. Late on Tuesday, the partial lists started to appear outside the White Star Office. Some of the names were even posted wrong!

MRS. A. E. LEWIS. It went on all day and all night. I couldn't sleep or rest, of course. Hundreds of families crowded the streets daily. This went on all week like that. I never knew till Friday that my husband was saved.

D. CROSS. My grandmother said to her class "Stand up any child who has a relative on the Titanic." And the whole class stood up. One little mite said "Oh, there's no need to worry, Miss, the Olympic is rushing to her aid." That's the trust of a child, isn't it?

S. TOWNSEND. London had received the complete first class lists two days earlier.

(D. CROSS continues on, quietly underscoring S. TOWNSEND'S next line. D. CROSS should give emphasis on phrases "lost her. . .")

D. CROSS. Mrs. May across the way lost her husband and oldest son. Mrs. Allen around the corner lost her husband, George. A young girl named Mrs. Barnes lost her brother, who was a fireman. Mrs. Gosling lost a son. And Mrs. Preston of Princes Street, a widow, lost her son too . . .

S. TOWNSEND. When all was said and done, nearly every road in Southampton had at least one person who had died on the Titanic. There were a total of 549 men lost, leaving 232 widows, and 1,200 children made orphans. Just like that, overnight, all these working class families without a provider. The grief was inescapable.

*(BLACKOUT. **ENSEMBLE** exits. Short MUSIC bridge. LIGHTS isolate **MRS. DOUGLAS** and **RUTH BECKER** talking together.)*

MRS. DOUGLAS. When we arrived in New York the crew of the Titanic was ordered to take off the recovered lifeboats before we could dock. I sat in a deck chair and listened and looked. The unseamanlike way of going at their simple tasks without excitement showed me more plainly than anything I had seen or heard the inefficiency of the crew.

RUTH BECKER. I remember leaving the Carpathia, walking down the gangway, and feeling so terribly embarrassed. I had borrowed a dress that was way too small and bursting at the seams. I must have been quite a sight! All the reporters came out in droves. They swarmed around us and poor Mother was so nervous when anybody asked her anything, she cried. She'd say, "Don't ask me, ask Ruth. She'll tell you."

*(LIGHTS isolate **MOLLY BROWN**. **MRS. DOUGLAS** and **RUTH BECKER** exit.)*

MOLLY BROWN. I helped the Red Cross find shelter for the needy and didn't leave the Carpathia until 3:00am that morning. As soon as I did, the press pounced upon me asking how I'd survived. My answer? "Typical Brown luck. I'm unsinkable."

*(LIGHTS shift. **MOLLY BROWN** exits.)*

THIRD CLASS. And so a legend was born. Many will never forget her.

FIRST CLASS. She was quite an inspiration, wouldn't you agree, Mr. Ismay?

ISMAY. So I understand.

THIRD CLASS. You can believe it! She went on to raise $10,000 for families of the sick and burial of the dead.

FIRST CLASS. She also served on the committee to make sure the White Star Line paid reparations.

THIRD CLASS. Which were very long in coming.

ISMAY. Yes, they were . . .

FIRST CLASS. Though at the time, reparations for the suffering was the furthest thing from your mind.

ISMAY. All I wanted to do was escape.

THIRD CLASS. Thankfully, that wasn't an option.

*(ISMAY reacts. Pause. **OFFICER, THIRD CLASS, FIRST CLASS** get close to **ISMAY**.)*

THIRD CLASS. The mourning reached far and wide in America and Europe.

OFFICER. From the 14,000 shipworkers in Belfast Ireland who built the Titanic–

FIRST CLASS. To the men on the Mackay-Bennett who retrieved the bodies.

THIRD CLASS. Everyone deeply felt the loss.

*(LIGHTS dim. SFX–tolling bells. LIGHTS isolate **FRED HAMILTON**.)*

F. HAMILTON. The tolling of the bells on the Mackay-Bennett summoned all hands to the boatdeck where 30 bodies are to be committed to the deep. Each carefully weighted, each carefully sewed up in canvas. It is a weird scene this gathering. For nearly an hour the words 'for as much as it hath pleased we therefore commit his body to the deep' are repeated. And at each throw comes a splash. Away the body plunges into the sea, there to sink to a depth of about 2 miles. Splash. Splash. Splash.

*(LIGHTS slowly shift back. **F. HAMILTON** exits.)*

OFFICER. In all, only 306 bodies were recovered.

FIRST CLASS. When the body of Eino Viljami Panul–a two-year old child–was found looking surprisingly untouched, even the toughest of the crew members wept openly.

THIRD CLASS. The seventy-five crew members adopted the child and paid for his funeral and headstone. Hundreds would later turn out for his funeral.

OFFICER. Meanwhile, everyone did what they could to go on with our lives.

FIRST CLASS. Most survivors managed to make a life for themselves after those first few difficult months.

OFFICER. For some, it took years.

THIRD CLASS. There were others who never recovered from the freezing sting of that remembered night.

OFFICER. The officers and crew, whose careers were so much a part of them, struggled to continue in their beloved trade.

ISMAY. Some of us quietly stayed hidden away from society.

*(LIGHTS shift and isolate **RUTH BECKER & EVA HART** talking.)*

EVA HART. My mother arranged passage back to England as our hopes of a new life in Canada died with my father. She never remarried.

RUTH BECKER. Life eventually went on for me, though like my mother, I refused to talk about the sinking for many years.

EVA HART. I understand completely. It took me years before I would ever speak of the disaster. Eventually, mother helped me to release those memories.

RUTH BECKER. *(Nods.)* My own children when they were young did not know I had been on the Titanic.

(LIGHTS isolate N. WILLIAMS. EVA HART and RUTH BECKER exit.)

N. WILLIAMS. My legs had been so badly frozen that the ship's physician recommended amputation and offered to do it. I absolutely refused and made a point to exercise them by walking every two hours, night and day. Gradually, they started to improve. But it took several months before I could resume my tennis career.

(LIGHTS isolate H. BRIDE. N. WILLIAMS exits.)

H. BRIDE. I had a short run as wireless operator on a steamer during World War I. After that, it took me ten years to return to the sea. The only job I could land was as wireless operator aboard the Cross-Channel Ferry. It was around that time I decide to disappear. I simply couldn't continue—too often someone would discover I was that Harold Bride of the Titanic. So I left London and moved to Glasgow, where I supported myself as a traveling salesman. I managed to cover my past so well, that even my own family did not know my true identity.

(LIGHTS isolate COLONEL GRACIE. H. BRIDE exits.)

COLONEL GRACIE. I was the first serious historian of the Titanic. Through correspondence with fellow passengers and crew I was able to collect stories for my book "The Truth about the Titanic".

FIRST CLASS. Colonel Gracie died just as his book was going to press.

*(LIGHTS isolate **MICHEL NAVRATIL. COLONEL GRACIE** exits.)*

M. NAVRATIL. Many years later I discovered my father's grave in Halifax, Nova Scotia.

(SFX music underscores.)

I put my hand on his gravestone, and I remembered that as a child, my father used to sing a lullaby, a Chopin etude, to my brother and I every night before we went to bed. And with my hand there on his gravestone, I could hear the angels singing that same lullaby.

*(LIGHTS isolate **LADY DUFF GORDON. M. NAVRATIL** exits.)*

LADY DUFF GORDON. Regrets? I have no regrets. The Titanic disaster made me a fortune. Look at the tremendous amount of publicity it gave me! When I opened my dress establishments in New York and Chicago, people mobbed the places. I made thousands and thousands of dollars.

*(LIGHTS isolate **OLDER LIGHTOLLER. LADY DUFF GORDON** exits.)*

OLDER LIGHTOLLER. I returned to work as soon as I could. They placed me back on the Oceanic where I remained until it struck a reef off the island of Foula and broke up. The only command I saw was a torpedo boat during my naval career in World War I. After the war, it became abundantly clear that White Star would never give me a command, so I retired from the sea. For several years I ran a guest house in London and raised chickens. Indeed yes, chickens! I continued to sail however, on the ship I designed and built—the Sundowner. During World War II, I had one more brush with adventure. My oldest son and I took the Sundowner to the battle of Dunkirk. Despite numerous bombing and strafing runs by Luftwaffe aircraft, we managed to save 130 men from the beaches.

*(LIGHTS isolate **J. THAYER. OLDER LIGHTOLLER** exits.)*

J. THAYER. I graduated from the University of Pennsylvania and made a name for myself in the banking business. Later I returned to my alma mater as the financial vice-president. I've never . . . I've never been able to erase the terrible visions of that night.

(LIGHTS shift.)

FIRST CLASS. After losing one of his sons in World War II, Jack Thayer succumbed to his haunted memories . . . and took his own life.

ISMAY. Dreadful . . .

*(**J. THAYER** exits.)*

THIRD CLASS. He was one of seven survivors to do so.

OFFICER. Who is to say how big a role the Titanic tragedy played in their decision?

*(LIGHTS shift and isolate **R. HARRIS**.)*

R. HARRIS. Well, I showed them all, didn't I? We already had the theatre on West 43rd Street and Henry had always depended on my "intuitive" input, so why not? I blazed ahead as Broadway's first woman producer. And if I do say so myself, I set the town afire! Remember, I was the one who discovered Moss Hart and produced his first play. Ah, those years were a such whirlwind! The '20s flew by in a blaze of success and splendor; including four more husbands—all of which were nothing more than momentary diversions. It was the crash of '29 that forever changed my cherished lifestyle. I lost everything, including my beloved theatre . . . By 1931 the last of my collected antiques were sold off and . . .

(Pause.)

I remember standing on the boat deck of the Titanic shortly after the collision. The third class passengers were milling around below toting everything they owned in trunks and suitcases. I remember thinking to myself: "Those poor souls! How dreadful it must be to see your life's possessions slipping out of your hands."

*(LIGHTS shift and isolate **MRS. DOUGLAS. R. HARRIS** exits.)*

MRS. DOUGLAS. Life slowly went on for me. My beloved Walter had made provisions so that I may continue to live comfortably. So my life became one of service, contributing and working with many philanthropic organizations—the Red Cross being my greatest interest. My cultural activities along with my fervent passion for writing helped to keep the grief manageable. Poetry became a great solace. I poured my heart onto the page to keep it intact . . .

*(LIGHTS shift back to **ISMAY, FIRST CLASS, THIRD CLASS** and **OFFICER. MRS. DOUGAS** exits.)*

ISMAY. All of these lives forever changed by . . . by decisions that I had a hand in making.

FIRST CLASS. Yes, Mr. Ismay.

*(LIGHTS shift to isolating **MRS. WHITE, MAJOR PEUCHEN,** and **EVA HART** in three different areas. They all look at **ISMAY** when speaking.)*

MRS. WHITE. Just to think that on a beautiful starlit night—you could see the stars reflected in the water—with all those Marconi warnings, that they would allow such an accident to happen, with such a terrible loss of life and property.

MAJOR PEUCHEN. I do criticize the policy and methods pursued by the company, for I feel sure that in this case caution would have been of every virtue and could have averted the terrible calamity.

EVA HART. This is the one disaster which there was no excuse for anyone to die. No one should have died. Had there been enough lifeboats in two and half hours in a very smooth sea—no one would have died. One life is worth more than a whole ship surely . . .

*(LIGHTS shift back. **MRS. WHITE, MAJOR PEUCHEN, EVA HART** exit.)*

ISMAY. Oh, God . . . We should have . . . We had a moral obligation to the people we served . . .

FIRST CLASS. An obligation that goes far and beyond the profits.

THIRD CLASS. Wouldn't you agree?

ISMAY. I . . . Yes . . . We had a golden opportunity to do what was . . . correct.

OFFICER. Instead, you chose the road of arrogance and greed.

ISMAY. God . . . No matter how hard I try, I cannot justify our actions.

THIRD CLASS. Then perhaps it is time for you to stop.

FIRST CLASS. Especially when confronted by the truth.

(Pause.)

ISMAY. How could I have allowed profits to become more important than human beings? It is almost unbearable...

FIRST CLASS. But you shall bear it, Mr. Ismay. It is part of your legacy.

ISMAY. I . . . I accept that now. God forgive me.

THIRD CLASS. The weight you carry leads you closer to what you seek.

*(**ISMAY** looks to the three spirits and they look back at him with compassion. LIGHTS dim. MUSIC "Nearer My God To Thee" underscores. The **OFFICER** gestures for **ISMAY** to come with him. **ISMAY** nods and takes a couple of steps following **OFFICER**. They are followed by **FIRST CLASS** and **THIRD CLASS**. **ISMAY** pauses a moment then offers his arm to **FIRST CLASS**. She smiles then steps back and guides **THIRD CLASS** to **ISMAY**. The two of them look at each other for a moment then **THIRD CLASS** takes his arm. They **ALL** proceed to exit together. LIGHTS slowly begin to fade out. SLIDE: LAWRENCE BEESLEY.)*

L. BEESLEY. *(VOICE OVER.)* Dusk fell as the Titanic pulled away from the dim and faint Irish mountains in the distance. So many experiences, both remarkable and unexpected, were yet to befall us before we saw land again. . .

(Slow BLACKOUT.)

CURTAIN

END OF PLAY

CAST OF CHARACTERS:

PRINCIPALS–

J. BRUCE ISMAY: Man. 74. Owner of the White Star Line at the time of the tragedy. Now near the end of his life and craving absolution.

FIRST CLASS: Woman (Edith Evans): Woman. 30s. One of the only four first class women to not survive. Now a spirit who has come to hold Ismay accountable.

THIRD CLASS: Woman 20s. Another casualty of the tragedy who has sought out Ismay to take responsibility for his part of the disaster and the treatment of the third class passengers.

OFFICER: (James P. Moody): Man. 20s. Also lost during the tragedy and wishes to have the truth exposed regarding the company's role in the disaster.

ENSEMBLE–*OPTIMUM* Casting 10 Women, 11 men:

Woman 1–20-30s. Edith Brown, Eva Hart, Leah Acks, Ensemble

Woman 2–20-30s. Ruth Becker, Anna Sofia Turja, Selena Cook, Katie Gilnaugh, Ensemble

Woman 3–20-30s. Newspaper Hawker 2, Dorothy Gibson, Marie Jerwan, Lady (off- stage, pg.71), Helen Bishop, Amy Stanley, Mrs. A .E. Lewis, Ensemble

Woman 4–25-40s. Luise Kink, Edith Russell, Mrs. Goldsmith, Ensemble

Woman 5–25-40s. Edwina Trout, Charlotte Collyer, Renee Harris, Ensemble

Woman 6–30-40s. Rhoda Abbott, Daisy Minahan, Dorothy Cross, Ensemble

Woman 7–35-50s. Elizabeth Lines, Margaret "Molly" Brown, Woman pg.86, Ruth Dodge, Ensemble

Woman 8–35-50s. Mrs. Stephenson, Mrs. Mahala Douglas, Mrs. Becker, Ensemble

Woman 9–40-50s. Emily Ryerson, Helen Candee, Lady Duff Gordon, Ensemble

Woman 10–40-50s. Mrs. J. Stuart White, Caroline Brown, Kate Buss, Ensemble

Man 1–20-30s. Newspaper Hawker 1, W. H. Taylor, Frank Prentice, Norman Chambers, Another Man pg.86, Frankie Goldsmith, Crewman pg.100, John Collins, Ensemble

Man 2–20-30s. Newspaper Hawker 3, Ernest Allen, G. A. Harder, Jack Ryerson, Jack Thayer, Carpathia First Officer, August Wennerstrom, Ensemble

Man 3–20-30s. Edward Buley, Karl Behr, Harold Bride, Crew Member 1 pg.79-94, Karl Midtsjo, Crewman pg.119-120, Stephen Townsend, Ensemble

Man 4–20-30s. Daniel Buckley, Frederick Fleet, Mr. Goldsmith, Harold Cottam, Robert Pusey, Man pg.130-131, John Thompson, Michel Navratil, Ensemble

Man 5–20-30s. John Hardy, Thomas Jones, Fred Barrett, Olaus Abelseth, Crew Member 2 pg. 79-94, Norris Williams, Ensemble

Man 6–30-50s. J. Bruce Ismay-1912, Frederick Clench, Frank Evans, Alfred Crawford, George Rheims, Charles Joughin, Robert Hitchens, Ensemble

Man 7–30-50s. Herbert Pitman, Harold Lowe, Capt. Stanley Lord, Steward pg.72-73 & 105-106, Mr. H. B. Harris, Fred Hamilton, Ensemble

Man 8–30-50s. Charles Lightoller, Older Charles Lightoller, Henry Etches, Eugene Daly, Man pg.122, Lawrence Beesley, Ensemble

Man 9–30-50s. Major A. G. Peuchen, George Moore, Capt. A. H. Rostron, Hugh Woolner, Charles Thomas, Crewman pg.134-136, Ensemble

Man 10–30-50s. Senator William Smith, Charles Stengel, Thomas Scanlan, Man pg.86, Mr. Theobald, Chief Engineer, Ensemble

Man 11–30-50s. Col. Archibald Gracie, Mr. George F. Crowe, Joseph Boxhall, Capt. J. H. Moore, Mr. Ryerson, Sir Duff Gordon, Ensemble

Extras

VOICE OVERS: **Female**–Mrs. Ida Straus. **Male**–Mr. Isidor Straus, Benjamin Guggenheim, Lord Mersey, Mr. Murdoch, Dr. W.F.N O'Loughlin, Capt. E. J. Smith, Man pg.68, Man pg.135.

ENSEMBLE–*MINIMUM* Casting 8 Women, 9 men:

Woman 1–20-30s. Edith Brown, Eva Hart, Mrs. Goldsmith, Woman pg.86, Leah Acks, Ensemble

Woman 2–20-30s. Anna Sofia Turja, Ruth Becker, Selena Cook, Katie Gilnaugh, Ensemble

Woman 3–20-30s. Newspaper Hawker 2, Dorothy Gibson, Marie Jerwan, Lady (off- stage, pg.71), Helen Bishop, Amy Stanley, Mrs. A .E. Lewis, Ensemble

Woman 4–25-40s. Luise Kink, Edwina Trout, Charlotte Collyer, Edith Russell, Renee Harris, Ensemble

Woman 5–35-50s. Elizabeth Lines,Margaret "Molly" Brown, Rhoda Abbott, Daisy Minahan, Ruth Dodge, Dorothy Cross, Ensemble

Woman 6–35-50s.Mrs. Mahala Douglas, Mrs. Becker, Mrs. Stephenson, Ensemble

Woman 7–40-50s. Emily Ryerson, Helen Candee, Lady Duff Gordon, Ensemble

Woman 8–40-50s. Mrs. J. Stuart White, Caroline Brown, Kate Buss, Ensemble

Man 1–20-30s. Newspaper Hawker 1, W. H. Taylor, Frank Prentice, Norman Chambers, Another Man pg.86, Frankie Goldsmith, Crewman pg.100, John Collins, Man pg.130-131, Ensemble

Man 2–20-30s. Newspaper Hawker 3, Ernest Allen, G. A. Harder, Jack Ryerson, Jack Thayer, Carpathia First Officer, August Wennerstrom, Ensemble

Man 3–20-30s. Mr. George F. Crowe, Karl Behr, George Moore, Harold Bride, Crew Member 1 pg.79-94, Karl Midtsjo, Crewman pg.125, Stephen Townsend, Ensemble

Man 4–20-30s. Daniel Buckley, Olaus Abelseth, John Hardy, Frederick Fleet, Fred Barrett, Crew Member 2 pg.79-94 *(Note, actor will leave the stage twice to become other characters)*, Mr. Goldsmith, Harold Cottam, Robert Pusey, John Thompson, Michel Navratil, Ensemble.

Man 5–20-30s. J. Bruce Ismay-1912, Frederick Clench, Thomas Jones, Hugh Woolner, Frank Evans, Alfred Crawford, George Rheims, Charles Joughin, Robert Hitchens, Ensemble

Man 6–30-50s. Herbert Pitman, Harold Lowe, Capt. Stanley Lord, Steward pg.72-73 & 105-106, Mr. H. B. Harris, Fred Hamilton, Ensemble

Man 7–30-50s. Charles Lightoller, Older Charles Lightoller, Capt. A. H. Rostron, Man pg.68, Henry Etches, Eugene Daly, Charles Thomas, Lawrence Beesley, Ensemble

Man 8–30-50s. Senator William Smith, Charles Stengel, Thomas Scanlan, Man pg.86, Mr. Theobald, Chief Engineer, Ensemble

Man 9–30-50s. Edward Buley,Major A. G. Peuchen, Joseph Boxhall, Capt. J. H. Moore, Col. Archibald Gracie, Mr. Ryerson, Norris Williams, Sir Duff Gordon, Man pg.122, Ensemble

Extras

VOICE OVERS: **Female**–Mrs. Ida Straus. **Male**–Mr. Isidor Straus, Benjamin Guggenheim, Lord Mersey, Mr. Murdoch, Dr. W.F.N O'Loughlin, Capt. E. J. Smith, Man pg.68, Man pg.135.

FOR PERFORMANCE RIGHTS

Please Contact:
Engelhardt Publishing
P.O. Box 820165
Portland, OR 97282

WEBSITE:
www.titanicaftermath.com

E-MAIL:
info@titanicaftermath.com

Character	Age at time of disaster	Gender	Nationality
WOMEN			
First Class Woman (Miss Edith Evans)	36	Female	America, New York City
Third Class Woman (unknown)	20s	Female	Actor's Choice
Abbott, Rhoda	39	Female	Born in Britain, Lived in U.S.
Acks, Leah	18	Female	Born in Poland, Lived in England
Becker , Ruth	12	Female	British, moved to America
Becker, Mrs. Nellie E.	35	Female	British, moved to America
Bishop, Helen	19	Female	American, Michigan
Brown , Caroline	59	Female	American, Massachusetts
Brown , Margaret "Molly"	44	Female	American, Born in Missouri, Lived in Denver
Brown, Edith	15	Female	South African British
Buss, Kate	36	Female	British, Kent
Candee, Helen	53	Female	American, Washington D.C.
Collyer, Charlotte	31	Female	British, Hampshire
Cook, Selena	22	Female	British, Oxford
Cross, Dorothy	30s	Female	British, Southampton
Dodge, Ruth	34	Female	American, San Francisco
Douglas, Mahala D.	48	Female	American, Minnesota
Gibson, Dorothy	22	Female	American, New York
Gilnagh, Katie	16	Female	Irish, Esker
Goldsmith, Mrs.	31	Female	Kent, England, moved to Detroit
Gordon, Lady Duff	48	Female	British, London
Harris, Renee	35	Female	American, New York
Hart, Eva	7	Female	British, London

Jerwan, Marie	23	Female	Swiss, moved to New York
Kink, Lusie	26	Female	Swiss
Lady (off-stage)	Any	Female	Any
Lewis , Mrs. A. E.	20s	Female	British, Southampton
Lines, Elizabeth	50	Female	American, New Jersey. Lived in Paris
Minahan, Daisy	33	Female	American, Wisconsin
Russell, Edith	33	Female	American, Ohio
Ryerson, Mrs. Emily	48	Female	American, Pennsylvania
Stanley, Amy	24	Female	British, Oxfordshire
Stephenson, Mrs. Martha	52	Female	American, Harvard
Straus, Mrs. Ida	63	Female	German, moved to U.S.
Trout, Edwina	27	Female	Born in Bath England, moved to America
Turja, Anna Sofia	18	Female	Finland, Oulu
White , Mrs. J. Stuart	55	Female	American, New York
Woman	Any	Female	Any
MEN			
Ismay, J. Bruce	74	Male	British, Crosby Liverpool
Officer (James P. Moody)	24	Male	British, Lincolnshire
Abelseth, Olaus	25	Male	Norwegian, moved to N.Dakota
Allen, Ernest	24	Male	British, Southampton
Barrett, Fred	20	Male	British, Liverpool
Beesley, Lawrence	34	Male	British, London
Behr, Karl	26	Male	American, New York
Boxhall , Joseph	38	Male	British, Yorkshire
Bride, Harold	22	Male	British, Southampton
Buckley, Daniel	24	Male	Irish, King Williamstown
Buley, Edward John	20	Male	British, Southampton
Carpathia First Officer	35	Male	British, Hampshire

(Horace J. Dean)			
Chambers, Norman C.	27	Male	America, New York City
Chief Engineer, Carpathia (A. B. Johnston)	59	Male	British
Clench, Frederick	35	Male	British, Southampton
Collins , John	17	Male	Irish, Belfast
Cottam, Harold	21	Male	British, Notts
Crawford, Alfred	36	Male	British, Southampton
Crew Member 1	Any	Male	British
Crew Member 2	Any	Male	British
Crewman	Any	Male	British
Crowe, George	30	Male	British, Southampton
Daly, Eugene	29	Male	Irish, Westmeath
Etches, Henry	41	Male	British, Southampton
Evans, Frank	27	Male	British, Southampton
Fleet, Frederick	24	Male	British, Southampton
Goldsmith, Frankie	9	Male	British, Kent. Moved to Detroit
Goldsmith, Mr.	33	Male	British, Kent. Moved to Detroit
Gordon , Sir Duff	49	Male	British, London
Gracie, Col. Archibald	54	Male	American, Washington D.C.
Guggenheim, Mr. Benjamin	46	Male	American, New York
Hamilton, Fred	30	Male	Unknown
Harder, G. A.	25	Male	America, New York City
Hardy, John	36	Male	British, Southampton
Harris, Mr. H. B.	45	Male	America, New York City
Hitchens, Robert	30	Male	British, Cornwall
Ismay, J. Bruce (1912)	49	Male	British, Crosby
Jones, Thomas	32	Male	British, Liverpool
Joughin, Charles	30	Male	British, Southampton

Lightoller, Charles H.	38	Male	British, Hampshire
Lightoller, Charles H. (older)	60s	Male	British, Hampshire
Lord, Capt. Stanley	35	Male	British, Bolton
Lowe, Harold	28	Male	Wales, Conwy
Man	Any	Male	Any
Man (off-stage)	Any	Male	Any
Man, Another	Any	Male	Any
Mersey, Lord	72	Male	British, London
Midtsjo, Carl	21	Male	Norwegian, Krakstad
Moore , Capt. James H.	50	Male	British
Moore, George	51	Male	British, Southampton
Murdoch, Mr. - VOICE ONLY	39	Male	Scotland, Dumbries
Navratil, Michel	2	Male	French, Nice
O'Loughlin, Dr. W.F.N.	62	Male	Irish, Dublin
Peuchen, Maj. Arthur G.	52	Male	Canadian, Toronto
Pitman, Herbert John	34	Male	British, Somerset
Prentice, Frank	22	Male	British, Southampton
Pusey, Robert	24	Male	British, Southampton
Rheims, George	36	Male	French, Paris
Rostron , Capt. Arthur H.	42	Male	British, Lancashire
Ryerson, Jack	13	Male	America, New York
Ryerson, Mr.	61	Male	America, New York
Scanlan, Thomas	38	Male	Irish, Lived in London
Smith , Captain E. J.	62	Male	British, Southampton
Smith, William Alden - Senator	53	Male	American, Michigan
Stengel, Charles E. Henry	54	Male	American, New Jersey
Steward	Any	Male	British
Straus, Mr. Isador	67	Male	Bavaria, moved to U.S.
Taylor, W. H.	28	Male	British, Southampton

Thayer, Jack	17	Male	American, Pennsylvania
Theobold, Mr.	34	Male	British, Kent
Thomas, Charles	31	Male	Lebanon, Hardin
Thompson, John	35	Male	British, Liverpool
Townsend, Stephen	30s	Male	British, Southampton
Wennerstrom, August	27	Male	Swedish, Ystad. Moved to New York
Williams , Norris	21	Male	American, Boston
Woolner, Hugh	45	Male	British, London

7652077R00092

Printed in Great Britain
by Amazon.co.uk, Ltd.,
Marston Gate.